THE APOCALYPSE
THE UNVEILING

THE APOCALYPSE
THE UNVEILING

Rev. Raymond G. Cross

Copyright © Rev. Raymond G. Cross.

All rights reserved. No part of this book may be reproduced in any form or by any electronic or mechanical means, including information storage and retrieval systems, without permission in writing from the publisher, except by reviewers, who may quote brief passages in a review.

ISBN: 978-1-64669-981-0   (Paperback Edition)
ISBN: 978-1-64669-982-7   (Hardcover Edition)
ISBN: 978-1-64669-980-3   (E-book Edition)

Some characters and events in this book are fictitious. Any similarity to real persons, living or dead, is coincidental and not intended by the author.

Book Ordering Information

Phone Number: 347-901-4929 or 347-901-4920
Email: info@globalsummithouse.com
Global Summit House
www.globalsummithouse.com

Printed in the United States of America

Contents

Preface ix
Note from the Author xv
Introduction xix

Chapter 1:   Revelation 1:1–3:22 1
Chapter 2:   Revelation 4:1–11:19 20
Chapter 3:   Revelation 12:1–13:18 50
Chapter 4:   Revelation 14:1–17:18 64
Chapter 5:   Revelation 18:1–22:21 87

Notes 113

I keep asking that the God of our Lord Jesus Christ, the glorious Father, may give you the Spirit of wisdom and revelation, so that you may know him better.

Ephesians 1:17

The LORD is compassionate and gracious, slow to anger, abounding in love. He will not always accuse, nor will he harbor his anger forever; he does not treat us as our sins deserve or repay us according to our iniquities. For as high as the heavens are above the earth, so great is his love for those who fear him; as far as the east is from the west, so far has he removed our transgressions from us. As a father has compassion on his children, so the LORD has compassion on those who fear him; for he knows how we are formed, he remembers that we are dust.

—Psalm 103:8–14

For the Lord Jesus Christ, who is the Father,
Son, and Holy Spirit (my prayer is that He will use this
work to glorify Himself), and also for my friend and fiancée,
Mary Ellen Joslin, as well as for her children, Suzanne James
and Jason Joslin, and their families.

PREFACE

> "For I know the plans I have for you," declares the LORD, "plans to prosper you and not to harm you, plans to give you hope and a future. Then you will call on me and come and pray to me, and I will listen to you. You will seek me and find me when you seek me with all your heart. I will be found by you,"
>
> —Jeremiah 29:11–13

To realize who God is, one has to study the Bible. We *only* know God by what *He tells us about Himself.* Studying the Scriptures reveals God's personality, psyche, and very being. In the process of showing Himself, God reveals His plan for humanity. Very much is learned about the self from God's Word. God is the great "I Am" (Yahweh). He is known as the "Self- Existent" and as the "Eternal One." The Scriptures say, "Hear, O Israel: The LORD our God, the LORD is one" (Deuteronomy 6:4). They also say, "Make every effort to keep the unity of the Spirit through the bond of peace. There is one body and one Spirit, just as you were called to one hope when you were called; one Lord, one faith, one baptism; one God and Father of all, who is over all and through all and in all. But to each one of us grace has been given as Christ apportioned it" (Ephesians 4:3–7).

Scriptural evidence indicates that God (Jesus Christ) divided Himself to be half-human and half-God. He did this so that He would be able to save humankind from its sins. Our Westminster Catechism asks in question 21, "Who is the redeemer of Gods elect?"

The answer is, "The only redeemer of God's elect is the Lord Jesus Christ, who, being the eternal Son of God, became man, and so was, and continues to be, God and man in two distinct natures, and one person, forever."

God divided Himself and became half-human so that He could experience His creation's life. God was literally able to live a human life to better judge humankind. Humankind has no excuse for its actions, because God as a human being was able to overcome all human shortcomings so that He could become our perfect, sinless sacrifice.

Even so, humankind *sins*. *Sin* figuratively means "missing the mark," as in an arrow missing the target. Sin is disobedience and evil to God. God *demands a sacrifice* to account for sin. Jesus became our perfect sacrifice, as God required, a requirement that Leviticus 14:19 details: "Then the priest is to sacrifice the sin offering and make atonement for the one to be cleansed from their uncleanness. After that, the priest shall slaughter the burnt offering." Note that the priest is to sacrifice the sin offering! Jesus is our prophet, as well as our High Priest and King, and He sacrificed Himself for our sins. Jesus, as our High Priest, offered Himself for our atonement and then had Himself slaughtered on the cross for us. Some Bibles translate this passage as "*kill* the burnt offering," but the original Hebrew word here means *slaughter* and is contracted to a root word, meaning *self*. That is exactly what Jesus did for us in giving Himself as a sacrifice for our sin debts.

These are God's regulations to meet His standards. He is our Creator, and His Word is law.

Why did God create the universe, animals, fish, birds, plants, water—everything—including humankind? David pondered the question of his being: "What is mankind that you are mindful of them, human beings that you care for them?" (Psalm 8:4).

Regardless of truth, human beings constantly make choices, whether spiritual (religious belief) or godly (the Bible and God's way) or physical (the sexual actions of gays and lesbians). The Bible is very clear regarding homosexuality in various verses, such as Leviticus 20:13, in which the Bible says, "If a man has sexual relations with a man as one does with a woman, both of them have done what is detestable. They are to be put to death; their blood will be on their own heads." And, speaking of homosexuality, we also read in the New Testament:

> Therefore God gave them over in the sinful desires of their hearts to sexual impurity for the degrading of their bodies with one another. They exchanged the truth about

God for a lie, and worshiped and served created things rather than the Creator—who is forever praised. Amen. Because of this, God gave them over to shameful lusts. Even their women exchanged natural sexual relations for unnatural ones. In the same way the men also abandoned natural relations with women and were inflamed with lust for one another. Men committed shameful acts with other men, and received in themselves the due penalty for their error. Furthermore, just as they did not think it worthwhile to retain the knowledge of God, so God gave them over to a depraved mind, so that they do what ought not to be done. (Romans 1:24–28)

The truth is that humankind has disregarded God for thousands of years, placing itself above God when it comes to decision making and self-control. Human beings have devised their own version of who they are, who their gods will be, and where they are going, leaving the true God completely out of the picture. Human beings have doomed themselves, choosing their own ways by leaving God out of their lives.

Human beings' mortal life and life after death are choices we make. In fact, the choice is yours to make as well! Obviously, *the correct choice is truth, to follow God and obey His instructions.*

Part of our manual for life is found in the Scriptures, and the rest comes when we accept Jesus as Lord and Savior. By accepting Jesus as Lord, God gives us a part of Himself, in the form of the Holy Spirit, who then guides, directs, and informs us, instructing us further with truth. The Bible communicates to us: "He [Jesus] is the one we proclaim, admonishing and teaching everyone with all wisdom, so that we may present everyone fully mature in Christ" (Colossians 1:28). The Bible, history, archeological findings, Noah's Ark on Mt. Ararat (it is there!), and many other truths found on earth and in the Bible exist as proof. The Bible has never been found to be in error! Human beings who refuse historical facts and the Bible choose not to believe God for His wondrous grace, mercy, and love, so they go their own way. God created everything for His benefit. It is God's plan that shapes the universe and not humankind's. It is only by God's Bible and His Holy Spirit that human beings have knowledge and wisdom concerning our future in God's plans. God tells us this in His Holy Word, the Bible: "This is what we speak, not in words taught us by human wisdom but in words taught by the Spirit, explaining spiritual realities with Spirit-taught words" (1 Corinthians 2:13).

Because of Satan, Adam and Eve became slaves to sin. We know from the Bible that sin is a horrible corruption of God's standards, because it is disobedience to God and to His righteousness, purity, holiness, and being. One of my previous books, *Scriptural Thoughts*, covers what sin looks like and what it does to people, but I will just mention a small portion of that subject here.

We know that after Jesus Christ was arrested, He was beaten, pummeled, whipped, scourged, battered, kicked, spat upon, and mocked, and he also had some of His beard pulled out and a crown of thorns placed on His head. Although bruised and bloody, *He still looked like a man.*

God had placed all our sins on Jesus when He went to the cross. As 2 Corinthians 5:21 tells us, "God made him who had no sin to be sin for us, so that in him we might become the righteousness of God." Hebrews 9:28 helps clarify this for us: "so Christ was sacrificed once to take away the sins of many; and he will appear a second time, not to bear sin, but to bring salvation to those who are waiting for him." So now we understand: *God had all sin, past, present and future placed on Jesus, on the cross.* Because of that fact, God described to Isaiah how He saw Jesus on the cross: "See, my servant will act wisely; he will be raised and lifted up and highly exalted. Just as there were many who were appalled at him—his appearance was so disfigured beyond that of any human being and his form marred beyond human likeness—" (Isaiah 52: 13–14). Christ Messiah, who was the perfect sinless one, took on Himself all of humankind's sins and actually became unrecognizable as a human being! That is what sin does to human beings.

Sin has condemned human beings to death, as we read in the book of Romans: "For the wages of sin is death, but the gift of God is eternal life in Christ Jesus our Lord" (Romans 6:23). Our dictionaries tell us that death is the cessation of mortal life. However, death, in the biblical sense, is *not* cessation of life! Death is an ongoing event of "ungodly Spiritual life." Death (the wages of sin) *is a permanent separation from God*, alive, in the lake of fire.

The Greek word for death is *thanatos* (θάνατος), which implies in the original language a total mortal death, figuratively and literally. However, *death, in the biblical sense, implies a living eternal Hell* for the person's living spiritual being. Death is the wage or payment for sin and it is a *separation* from God (from all that is righteous and good).

How does one correct this situation? Ezekiel 18:31 tells us: "Rid yourselves of all the offenses you have committed, and get a new heart and a new spirit." The Bible later tells us, "Jesus answered, 'Very truly I tell you, no one can enter the kingdom of God unless they are born of water and the Spirit'" (John 3:5). Another relevant verse comes from the book of Job: "But it is the spirit in a person, the breath of the Almighty, that gives them understanding" (32:8). The Scriptures further advise:

> For if we have been united with him in a death like his, we will certainly also be united with him in a resurrection like his. For we know that our old self was crucified with him so that the body ruled by sin might be done away with, that we should no longer be slaves to sin—because anyone who has died has been set free from sin. Now if we died with Christ, we believe that we will also live with him. For we know that since Christ was raised from the dead, he cannot die again; death no longer has mastery over him. The death he died, he died to sin once for all; but the life he lives, he lives to God. In the same way, count yourselves dead to sin but alive to God in Christ Jesus. Therefore do not let sin reign in your mortal body so that you obey its evil desires. Do not offer any part of yourself to sin as an instrument of wickedness, but rather offer yourselves to God as those who have been brought from death to life; and offer every part of yourself to him as an instrument of righteousness. For sin shall no longer be your master, because you are not under the law, but under grace. What then? Shall we sin because we are not under the law but under grace? By no means! Don't you know that when you offer yourselves to someone as obedient slaves, you are slaves of the one you obey—whether you are slaves to sin, which leads to death, or to

obedience, which leads to righteousness? But thanks be to God that, though you used to be slaves to sin, you have come to obey from your heart the pattern of teaching that has now claimed your allegiance. You have been set free from sin and have become slaves to righteousness. I am using an example from everyday life because of your human limitations. Just as you used to offer yourselves as slaves to impurity and to ever-increasing wickedness, so now offer yourselves as slaves to righteousness leading to holiness. When you were slaves to sin, you were free from the control of righteousness. What benefit did you reap at that time from the things you are now ashamed of? Those things result in death! But now that you have been set free from sin and have become slaves of God, the benefit you reap leads to holiness, and the result is eternal life. For the wages of sin is death, but the gift of God is eternal life in Christ Jesus our Lord. (Romans 6:5–23)

* * * * *

One distinctive feature in the whole Bible is the number seven. This number is the most used number in the Scriptures; it appears 461 times. Forty is the next most popular number, appearing 115 times. The general meaning of scriptural numbers is defined in one of my previous books, *Scriptural Thoughts*. For our purposes here, let us note that the book of Revelation contains thirty-one sevens. Eighteen of the sevens mentioned include the seven churches, seven spirits, seven lampstands, seven stars, seven seals, a lamb with seven horns and seven eyes, seven trumpets, seven thunders, seven signs, a dragon with seven heads and seven crowns, a leopard-beast with seven heads, a scarlet-like beast with seven heads, seven plagues, seven mountains, seven kings, and seven new things. Also included among the thirty-one sevens are seven of Revelation's beatitudes. These blessings are found in Revelation 1:3, 14:13, 16:15, 19:9, 20:6, 22:7, and 22:14. To God, the number seven is a perfect completion number.

* * * * *

Note from the Author

> The fear of the LORD is the beginning of knowledge, but fools despise wisdom and instruction.
>
> —Proverbs 1:7

In 1966, my life changed dramatically. I worked for IBM as a design engineer in the advanced technology group. In 1966, I received Jesus as my Lord and Savior to become a saved person—*born again*—via the Bible's truths. My scientific-engineering existence and *my worldview* changed, and I needed to undo a great deal of learning, literally *unlearning many false teachings* regarding religious belief and thought. I needed to separate myself from half-truths and/or false truths, and having no religion or belief requires diligent study—*study seeking the truth*. If you are reading this and are not a true believer in Jesus Christ as Lord and Savior, perhaps you need to relearn or to unlearn some of your teachings.

After years of studying the Bible, history, commentaries, and archeological findings, I took early retirement from IBM. I went to Reformed Seminary in Clinton, Mississippi and I became a minister of the gospel in the Presbyterian Church in America. My first and only church was the Sardis Presbyterian Church in America. After twenty-seven years, I retired and have published two other books: *Scriptural Thoughts* and *Words to Think About*. Lord willing, I plan one more book after this one, the book of beginnings known as Genesis.

It is with great trepidation I write this work concerning the book of Revelation. Why, one may ask? Because God conveys the following warning words to us: "And if anyone takes words away from this scroll of prophecy, God will take away from that person any share in the tree of life and in the Holy City, which are described in this scroll" (Revelation 22:19).

The term *revelation* is taken from the Greek word *apocalypse* (ἀποκάλυψε), meaning the unveiling or the uncovering—the revealing. This writer acknowledges the Bible as total truth and owes very much to numerous spiritual men before him who have dedicated their lives to understanding what God has ordained. Great ministers and writers, such as John, Paul, Matthew, Dr. Luke, Isaiah, Moses, David, and many other biblical writers, have shown the truth, for all to receive. I would also have to include other men, such as Matthew Poole, Matthew Henry, Herbert W. Armstrong, H. L. Willmington, Arno C. Gaebalien, F. W. Grant, J. Vernon McGee, and many others too numerous to mention. Reading the Scriptures, writings by these men, and texts about historical findings, has influenced this writer to present biblical knowledge so that people might have better understanding of God and His book. Some of the aforementioned men's thoughts, combined with the study of God's Holy Word and *unfathomable* help from the Holy Spirit, triggered this cognitive content meant to give readers a better understanding of life—not only mortal, but also immortal life. This work's prime purpose is for humankind to truly realize its future in God's program.

The Bible and the book of Revelation remain misunderstood, because *human beings reject God*. Human beings, throughout time, have rejected the truth given to them, beginning with the very first verse of the Bible: "… God created the heavens and the earth" (Genesis 1:1). *Rather than accept the truth*, humankind imagines itself wise enough to figure out its existence by evolution, incarnation, or other means. Human beings have always wanted to live forever and have devised various religious beliefs and practices to attempt to implement their shallow thinking. The interesting thing is that human beings do live eternally, but they either do so with God or completely separately from Him. In any case, human beings do live eternally.

No person is wise enough to grasp the holiness, purity, and wonder of our fantastically loving God! Nor can anyone ever understand the love given to him or her by God. However, one day human beings will know the truth of the Bible and the book of Revelation, either in eternal "death" or eternal spiritual life. Christ is coming and—I add—that day is fast approaching. God

Himself wrote this book as a warning to all humanity! The Scriptures tell us, "We also have the prophetic message as something completely reliable, and you will do well to pay attention to it, as to a light shining in a dark place, until the day dawns and the morning star rises in your hearts. Above all, you must understand that no prophecy of Scripture came about by the prophet's own interpretation of things. For prophecy never had its origin in the human will, but prophets, though human, spoke from God as they were carried along by the Holy Spirit" (2 Peter 1:19–21). God has ordained His will for salvation, redemption, and finality for humankind. All of God's plans will happen, just as all of the 333 specific prophetic details pertaining to Christ's first coming occurred.[1] I might add that those prophesies were completed against impossible astronomical odds.

God's resolve, His will, His intent, and His purpose will prevail in all matters. He has informed us of His thoughts and witness to all events. All one has to do is read His Word to learn and understand God's total design for humanity from day one: "Ask now about the former days, long before your time, from the day God created human beings on the earth; ask from one end of the heavens to the other. Has anything so great as this ever happened, or has anything like it ever been heard of?" (Deuteronomy 4:32).

Most men have disregarded God's witness of over six thousand years of human life on earth, and theologians believe we are definitely in the last days of time—an era that began when Christ was on the cross. More importantly, we are entering the beginning of the "tribulation" period. What does "last days" really mean? Several Bible prophets have told us what to expect, and current events strengthen the Bible's prophecy.

Revelation tells us very much about all that will occur during the beginning of the tribulation, the rapture, and during the "great tribulation." Time will end with the final coming of our Lord and Savior, Jesus Christ. Do not be like the obstinate people who will not believe the truth! The Scriptures say, "But because of your stubbornness and your unrepentant heart, you are storing up wrath against yourself for the day of God's wrath, when his righteous judgment will be revealed" (Romans 2:5).

Read the Bible, think about its teaching, and ask the Lord into your heart as the book of Romans tells us,

> But what does it say? "The word is near you; it is in your mouth and in your heart," that is, the message concerning faith that we proclaim: If you declare with your mouth, "Jesus is Lord," and believe in your heart that God raised him from the dead, you will be saved. For it is with your heart that you believe and are justified, and it is with your mouth that you profess your faith and are saved. As Scripture says, "Anyone who believes in him will never be put to shame." For there is no difference between Jew and Gentile—the same Lord is Lord of all and richly blesses all who call on him, for, "Everyone who calls on the name of the Lord will be saved." (Romans 10:8–13)

* * * * *

Introduction

> Surely the Sovereign LORD does nothing without revealing his plan to his servants the prophets.
>
> —*Amos 3:7*

The Bible is the most wonderful book ever communicated to human beings. About forty-five different people wrote the Bible over a period of about fifteen hundred years. Although it was written in different eras, by writers of different backgrounds, education, and family culture, each book in the Bible dovetails with every other book, as if—*as if*—one author wrote it. In fact, one author *did*! God oversaw the writing of His great book! Thousands of written books try to fathom the realities of God's words. The book of The Revelation actually depicts the final fulfillment of God's prophecies and plans for humanity.

This book, *The Apocalypse: The Unveiling*, is an attempt to condense the meanings of the book of the Revelation's information. By doing this, this book reveals some of the symbolic meanings of Revelation's prophecy in order to make it easier to understand humankind's position in God's plans. *My purpose in writing this book is to warn humankind that Jesus is coming soon.* Most theological scholars believe we have entered the pre-tribulation period mentioned as "birth pains" by Jesus. Jesus spoke to us concerning this period in Matthew: "Jesus answered: 'Watch out that no one deceives you. For many will come in my name, claiming, 'I am the Messiah,' and will deceive many. You will hear of wars and rumors of wars, but see to it that you are not alarmed. Such things must happen, but the end is still to come. Nation will rise against nation, and kingdom against kingdom. There will be famines and earthquakes in various places. All these are the beginning of birth pains'" (Matthew 24:4–8). The "birth pains" mentioned here refer to the beginning of the "tribulation period." The word *tribulation* appears only a couple of times in Scripture. Revelation 7:14 offers us one of those times: "I answered, 'Sir, you know.' And he said, 'These are they who have come out of the great tribulation; they have washed their robes and made them white in the blood of the Lamb.'"

The tribulation starts with the change in weather patterns, enhanced earthquakes, and an increase in hurricanes, tornadoes, tsunamis, cold, heat, drought, floods, snow, rainstorms, and active volcanoes. It also starts with wars, terrorism, human corruption, and other signs of evil and violence increasing. The tribulation will continue to run its course with increasing intensity until Christ returns.

Many Theologians and scholars believe this period is here, because in the past, God would begin chastising Israel by bringing calamity and disaster of various kinds. One of the great prophesies to consider regarding this era of time is in book of Matthew, where Jesus cautions us, "But about that day or hour no one knows, not even the angels in heaven, nor the Son, but only the Father. As it was in the days of Noah, so it will be at the coming of the Son of Man" (Matthew 24:36–37). *What was it like in Noah's day?* Noah's day was only 1,676 years from Adam and Eve's time on earth. That number results from simple addition that takes into account the generations given from Adam to Noah (and the flood) found in Genesis 5. Genesis 6:5 tells us: "The LORD saw how great the wickedness of the human race had become on the earth, and that *every inclination of the thoughts of the human heart was only evil all the time.*" In addition, Genesis 6:11–14 informs us, "Now *the earth was corrupt in God's sight and was full of violence. God saw how corrupt the earth had become*, for all the people on earth had corrupted their ways. So God said to Noah, 'I am going to put an end to all people, *for the earth is filled with violence* because of them. I am surely going to destroy both them and the earth. So make yourself an ark of cypress wood; make rooms in it and coat it with pitch inside and out.'" (emphasis added)

We see *more violence and corruption today* than at any other time in history. Think about some of what happens today. The world has seen more wars in the last one hundred years than in all of history.

Volcanic eruption has multiplied more in the last fifty years than ever before. Earthquakes are becoming more numerous and more amplified, causing tsunamis and other disasters. Weather patterns are playing havoc with crops and water supplies, and destruction by tornadoes, drought, cold, and heat instability make some proclaim *and blame* humankind for its cause. Humankind is also experiencing *unprecedented corruption and violence* in the world. We see violence in the media, TV shows, the streets, schools, industry, and sports. More shootings occur in our country now than did in the old Wild West. And do not forget the *violence* of over *55 million abortions in our country alone*. I believe Jesus is coming soon, simply by *comparing our day to Noah's day*.

In addition to the above, we see more anti-Semitic and anti-Christian occurrences worldwide, becoming the vogue. *The Baptist Record* recently reported that 75 percent of nations now abuse Christians and Jews. That figure does not *fully account* for the radical Muslims beheading or killing anyone who is not a believer in their false god, Allah. Many people are not interested in and do not believe in the true God, so Christ's coming will be a surprise.

The book of Revelation deals with humankind's prophetic time on earth, depicting the finality of our fate, when Christ comes. The author is Jesus, as is testified by the book's first verse. The information came in visions to John, the "beloved," when he was a prisoner on the Isle of Patmos, believed to be a Roman prison. The book of Revelation was written somewhere between AD 86 and AD 95, after John was released from Patmos.

The book of Revelation was *written as a letter to the seven churches* to encourage them, because they were persecuted and suffered under the Romans. The early church of Christians underwent terrible persecutions beginning in John's time, but the early church was also suffering from corruption and apostasy *from within*. Imperial Rome, under its vicious leadership, attempted to eliminate Christianity by killing, crucifying, throwing people to wild animals, hand fighting to the death, and other means of slaughter. All of this and many other horrible deeds took place as spectators watched.

Revelation 1–3 gives us "The Things which are." This is an account of John's day, and it includes an opening statement, greetings, and this letter to the seven churches. However, as we shall see, these seven churches' actions very closely resemble an explanatory history of Christ's existing churches on earth.

Chapters 4–12 tell us of "The Things to come." These chapters cover what is to occur in the very near future.

Theologically, the book of Revelation is comprehended in several different ways. There are the "preterist," the "historical," the "futurist," and the "spiritualist" views or interpretations. Very simply expressed, the preterist interpretation sees Revelation as referring only to John's day. The historical interpretation covers all of Christianity, or the church period. The futurist viewpoint sees only the time of the Lord's coming and the end of the world for humankind. Moreover, the spiritualist interpretation sees only greatly figurative, pictorial language representing a divine government led by Jesus, which is applicable to all of time and eternity. In actuality, I believe all of the above (and more) could easily apply to this great book.

Jesus introduces us to the birth pains, the beginning of the great tribulation, with these words from Matthew 24:21–25: "For then there will be great distress, unequaled from the beginning of the world until now—and never to be equaled again. If those days had not been cut short, no one would survive, but for the sake of the elect those days will be shortened. At that time if anyone says to you, 'Look, here is the Messiah!' or, 'There he is!' do not believe it. For false messiahs and false prophets will appear and perform great signs and wonders to deceive, if possible, even the elect. See, I have told you ahead of time."

God's wrath does not fall on His children, but there will be suffering for some of those who are believers in Christ Jesus as Lord. One may ask why God is bringing these catastrophic events to the world and to the United States at this time. First, it is part of God's plan, and second, *it results from humankind's disobedience of God.* The world is in chaos, with greed, corruption, and evil changing the truth to lies and violence. America has killed (and continues to kill) millions of babies with abortion laws. *What idiot proclaimed that a fetus is not human until the month someone designates it as human?* I attest to anyone with common sense that a human female embryo united with a human male sperm produces a human being, not a blob! Even worse is the fact that many people have *endorsed* this travesty of truth, this outright lie! With all of this violence, God is totally left out and unwanted by humanity, because human beings wish to rule themselves.

The United States, England, New Zealand, Australia, and many other once great nations will go down, and it is starting to happen, because God is closing out time. That is why, to repeat, *this book is a warning for all of humankind*. God, from millennial time, has shown humankind that He is coming again. Human beings leave God out of their lives and pay no attention to His admonitions. Jesus will fulfill His prophecy to come again, but just as the flood was, His coming will be a surprise to many.

Understand that from time immemorial, humankind has *devised* religions that are not true and do not honor God in any form. Christianity is not a religion, but Christians are followers of Christ. The only way to honor God is to do things His way! In other words, there is only one correct belief in a true God, and all the others are false. Christianity is not *only about faith but also a relationship with God*. Humankind is receiving its last chance to *repent* (a Greek word meaning to think differently) and obey God.

* * * * *

1

REVELATION 1:1–3:22

> For prophecy never had its origin in the human will, but prophets, though human, spoke from God as they were carried along by the Holy Spirit.
>
> —2 Peter 1:21

Try to remain on unbiased ground when reading the book of Revelation. Please likewise approach this book, *The Apocalypse: The Unveiling,* with an open mind. *This presentation is a neutral rendition using many exegeses of the Bible, with much thought and help* from the Holy Spirit. It is an attempt to clarify some thoughts—ideas by learned men and women—using spiritual insights from the Holy Spirit. May the reader study further and draw his or her own conclusions.

Revelation 1:1–2

According to Revelation 1:1–2, "The revelation from Jesus Christ, which God gave him to show his servants what must soon take place. He made it known by sending his angel to his servant John, who testifies to everything he saw—that is, the word of God and the testimony of Jesus Christ." These first two verses testify that Jesus is the author and that John was the writer for Him.

Revelation 1:3

Revelation 1:3 is the first of *seven* beatitudes or blessings found in the book of Revelation: "Blessed is the one who reads aloud the words of this prophecy, and blessed are those who hear it and take to heart what is written in it, because the time is near." These blessings are a confirmation of the eight blessings found in Matthew 5:3–11. Blessings always bring joy, especially those which come to man from God Himself.

Revelation 1:4–5a

Jesus addresses John and the seven churches of that time in Revelation 1:4– 5a: "John, To the seven churches in the province of Asia: Grace and peace to you from him who is, and who was, and who is to come, and from the seven spirits before his throne, and from Jesus Christ, who is the faithful witness, the firstborn from the dead, and the ruler of the kings of the earth." He also restates that He (Jesus) is the only true faithful witness, the firstborn from the dead, and the only King of Kings.

The seven churches—Ephesus, Smyrna, Pergamum, Thyatira, Sardis, Philadelphia, and Laodicea—were in Asia Minor, within approximately a hundred-mile radius of each other. There were other churches in Asia Minor and Turkey, but apparently these seven churches comprised choice Roman centers, because they stood on the main roads. These churches, probably by their placement, were substantially organized and relatively large. In addition, the seven churches appear to be forecasts, prophesy concerning Jesus historical church on earth.

Revelation 1:5b–8

Jesus identifies Himself as the one "who is, and who was, and who is to come, the Almighty" in Revelation 1:5b–8: "To him who loves us and has freed us from our sins by his blood, and has made us to be a kingdom and priests to serve his God and Father—to him be glory and power for ever and ever! Amen. 'Look, he is coming with the clouds,' and 'every eye will see him, even those who pierced him'; and all peoples on earth 'will mourn because of him.' So shall it be! Amen. 'I am the Alpha and the Omega,' says the Lord God, 'who is, and who was, and who is to come, the Almighty.'" Verse 7 says, "Every eye will see him, even those who pierced him, and all peoples on earth." This vision of Jesus pertains to His coming to earth at the very end and not His coming in the clouds at rapture time. This assumption comes about because the following prediction for Israel occurs, when the Lord comes at the very end of time and touches the earth: "And I will pour out on the house of David and the inhabitants of Jerusalem a spirit of grace and supplication. They will look on me, the one they have pierced, and they will mourn for him as one mourns for an only child, and grieve bitterly for him as one grieves for a firstborn son" (Zechariah 12:10). All living people (and, perhaps, all of those longtime dead) will see and recognize Jesus when He comes at the end of time. Jesus reiterates He is the first and the last, "the Alpha and the Omega." Jesus is the only one who can claim that title, and He is the Lord of Lords and King of Kings.

Revelation 1:9–11

Then, in verses 9 through 11, John writes the visions given to him: "I, John, your brother and companion in the suffering and kingdom and patient endurance that are ours in Jesus, was on the island of Patmos because of the word of God and the testimony of Jesus. On the Lord's Day I was in the Spirit, and I heard behind me a loud voice like a trumpet, which said: 'Write on a scroll what you see and send it to the seven churches: to Ephesus, Smyrna, Pergamum, Thyatira, Sardis, Philadelphia and Laodicea.'" These seven churches of John's day foretell the chronological characteristics of the earthly churches' historical account.

Revelation 1:12–18

John ends the opening statement in verses 12 to 18 by telling us,

> I turned around to see the voice that was speaking to me. And when I turned I saw seven golden lampstands, and among the lampstands was someone like a son of man, dressed in a robe reaching down to his feet and with a golden sash around his chest. The hair on his head was white like wool, as white as snow, and his eyes were like blazing fire. His feet were like bronze glowing in a furnace, and his voice was like the sound of rushing waters. In his right hand he held seven stars, and coming out of his mouth was a sharp, double-edged sword. His face was like the sun shining in all its brilliance. When I saw him, I fell at his feet as though dead. Then he placed his right hand on me and said: "Do not be afraid. I am the First and the Last. I am the Living One; I was dead, and now look, I am alive for ever and ever! And I hold the keys of death and Hades."

Here John sees Christ among His seven lampstands, His church of earthly history. This description—"the hair on his head was white like wool, as white as snow"—appears several times in Scripture. Here, from Daniel 7:9, is one of the references. "As I looked, thrones were set in place, and the Ancient of Days took his seat. His clothing was as white as snow; the hair of his head was white like wool. His throne was flaming with fire, and its wheels were all ablaze."

Jesus is the only true living God. He lives forever, eternally, and He alone has the keys to death and Hades.

Revelation 1:19–20

Revelation 1:12–20 gives us *a mental picture of Jesus Christ*, but John sees him symbolically as being *in and with* His churches. Literally, Jesus is with His churches (the lampstands) throughout human time, and these seven letters to seven churches are a preview of human beings' church chronicle. Toward the end of this preview come verses 19 and 20: "Then I wanted to know the meaning of the fourth beast, which was different from all the others and most terrifying, with its iron teeth and bronze claws—the beast that crushed and devoured its victims and trampled underfoot whatever was left. I also wanted to know about the ten horns on its head and about the other horn that came up, before which three of them fell—the horn that looked more imposing than the others and that had eyes and a mouth that spoke boastfully." Verse 19 tells John to write "what you have seen, what is now and what will take place later." This reflects the connection of time periods to John's day, human earthly life in the time left, and how human life will end.

One can easily see the association of the "seven lampstands" being representative of the seven churches, because *the church is the only giver of light to a lost and dying world*. The seven stars called the "angels" of the churches may refer to the pastors or leaders of local churches. The word *angel* actually translates as "messenger." In addition, remember that these seven church letters, these admonitions, and this prophecy pertained *not only to John's day but also to true church history*.

Dr. H. L. Willmington[1] had this to say about the seven churches: "The chronological purpose: That the charismatics of these churches serve as a prophetical preview of the seven great church periods in Christendom, from Pentecost to the rapture." Dr. Willmington's categorization follows, and most theologians agree with this classification. Study shows that it is very reasonable to assume the character of the seven churches of John's day were assimilated by the history of the church periods listed here:

- the church at Ephesus ("desirable"): about AD 30–100
- the church at Smyrna ("myrrh"; the martyr church): AD 100–313
- the church at Pergamum ("marriage"; compromising church): AD 313– 590
- the church at Thyatira ("continual sacrifice"; the Roman Catholic Church): AD 590–1517
- the church at Sardis ("remnant"; the Reformation church): AD 1517– 1700

- the church at Philadelphia ("brotherly love"; the revival church): AD 1700–1900
- the church at Laodicea (the "people's rights"; the worldly church): AD 1900–rapture?

* * * * *

Revelation 2:1–7

This brings us to our first church letter to Ephesus (which means "desirable"), the church period between AD 30 and 300:

> To the angel of the church in Ephesus write: These are the words of him who holds the seven stars in his right hand and walks among the seven golden lampstands. I know your deeds, your hard work and your perseverance. I know that you cannot tolerate wicked people, that you have tested those who claim to be apostles but are not, and have found them false. You have persevered and have endured hardships for my name, and have not grown weary. Yet I hold this against you: You have forsaken the love you had at first. Consider how far you have fallen! Repent and do the things you did at first. If you do not repent, I will come to you and remove your lampstand from its place. But you have this in your favor: You hate the practices of the Nicolai tans, which I also hate. Whoever has ears, let them hear what the Spirit says to the churches. To the one who is victorious, I will give the right to eat from the tree of life, which is in the paradise of God. (Revelation 2:1–7)

Five of the individual church letters state; "I know your works." Smyrna says;- "I know your "tribulation and poverty." Pergamum says; "I know where you dwell, Where Satan's throne is." Jesus describes the situation regarding churches of John's day, but the tragedy is that modern churches fit these same descriptions. Today's society and people are so busy with 'things' that they, with their 'works,' have neglected Christ. People are 'busy' and not very involved with our Christian heritage.

Christ's church was undergoing terrible evil and corruption in John's day, such as those caused by the Nicola itans (and others with false beliefs), who had crept in to usurp control. They were at Ephesus, and many ancient writers wrote about the Nicolai tans. For example,

> Irenaeus, in the 15th century wrote how the Nicola itans were the followers of Nicolas, who was one of the seven first ordained to be a leader in the early church by the apostles. The Nicolai tans lead lives of unrestrained indulgence. The character of these men is very plainly pointed out in the Apocalypse by John, [where they are represented] as teaching that it is a matter of indifference to sin and allows the practice of adultery as well as to eat things sacrificed to idols.

As early as the closing of the apostolic age, faith without works was one of the forms of error taught by unscrupulous men and women. Even James, the brother of Jesus, who was a pillar in the early Jerusalem church, wrote his book to put down this type of thinking: "You foolish person, do you want evidence that faith without deeds is useless?" (James 2:20).

The Nicolai tans believed in A*ntinomianism*, which had *corrupted the early church.* According to Merriam-Webster's Dictionary, an antinomian is "one who holds that under the gospel dispensation of grace the moral law is of no use or obligation because faith alone is necessary to salvation." Wikipedia further adds, "Many Antinomians, however, believe that *Christians will obey the moral law despite their freedom from it.* The distinction between Antinomian and other Christian views, on moral law is that, Antinomians believe that obedience to the law is motivated by an internal principle, flowing from belief rather than any external compulsion" (emphasis added).

The Antinomian believers claimed to have known Christ Jesus and to have had Jesus's approval for their teachings of indulgence of evil practices. This lie was to bring the church into their accord with immoral sexual and idol practices. Paul, in 1 Corinthians 6:9–11, describes very well the believers in Antinomianism: "Or do you not know that wrongdoers will not inherit the kingdom of God? *Do not be deceived: Neither the sexually immoral nor idolaters nor adulterers nor men who have sex with men nor thieves nor the greedy nor drunkards nor slanderers nor swindlers will inherit the kingdom of God.* And that is what some of you were. But you were washed, you were sanctified, you were justified in the name of the Lord Jesus Christ and by the Spirit of our God." (emphasis added)

Jesus commended the people of Ephesus for their evangelical works while also chastising them for falling away from the truth. This church was to repent and change their ways. The Ephesus church era provided the writing of the New Testament, which was a blessing to the whole world—especially to people who believe and have faith in Jesus Christ as Lord and Savior. Apparently, they did not truly repent ("think differently,"), because the Ephesus "lampstand" was removed as the harbor receded from the port. Ephesus is now several miles inland from the Mediterranean Sea.

Ephesus had one of the Seven Wonders of the World, the Temple of Diana. The Greek name for the temple was Artemis. According to J. Vernon McGee, this temple had over over one hundred columns that were fifty-six feet high, with thirty-six of them being hand carved. Columns and walls were Parian marble, with a staircase carved from one Cypress vine. Behind a purple curtain was a large idol image of Diana, the multi-breasted goddess of fertility.[2]

Ephesus was a large city of about 225,000 people. It had a huge harbor positioned ideally for trade, and the temple brought many tourists. The silversmith idol imagery mentioned in Acts 19:23–41 depicts an event with Paul. Ephesus was empirically typical of the church age until about AD 313. While the modern church period has held on to many true beliefs, falsehood and corruption crept in very early in the church's history.

* * * * *

Revelation 2:8–11

John's next letter was to the Smyrna church (meaning "myrrh"), also known as the martyr church, the church period extending from AD 100 to 313. In Colossians we read, "Now I rejoice in what I am suffering for you, and I fill up in my flesh what is still lacking in regard to Christ's afflictions, for the sake of his body, which is the church" (1:24). This leads us to Smyrna:

> To the angel of the church in Smyrna write: These are the words of him who is the First and the Last, who died and came to life again. I know your afflictions and your poverty—yet you are rich! I know about the slander of those who say they are Jews and are not, but are a synagogue of Satan. Do not be afraid of what you are about to suffer. I tell you, the devil will put some of you in prison to test you, and you will suffer persecution for ten days. Be faithful, even to the point of death, and I will give you life as your victor's crown. Whoever has ears, let them hear what the Spirit says to the churches. The one who is victorious will not be hurt at all by the second death. (Revelation 2:8–11)

These are the words of *the First and Last, who died and came to life again,* the Lord Jesus Christ. Smyrna was about forty miles from Ephesus on the same trade route, which went from India to Rome. Smyrna had schools of science, medicine, and engineering and was renowned for its beautiful buildings and architecture. There was also a temple for Bacchus, the god of wine, and many recreant Jews lived there. The people of Smyrna suffered hunger, poverty, financial loss, and martyrdom due to their belief in Christ. Satan was very powerful there and politically controlled the situation, so Jesus told them to remain faithful to secure the Victor's crown. There was a large contingent of hostile Jews who made it very difficult for Christians, because Smyrna politically aligned with Rome. History records Polycarp martyred there in AD 168, with the apostate Jews bringing the wood to have him burned at the stake. This church era saw over five million Christians killed by vicious, barbarian Roman emperors, who desired to wipe out Christianity.

The Smyrna epoch was typical of churches during the early period up to AD 325. Constantine gave rest to the churches from persecution, but many false doctrines and forms of corruption had become part of the early true church.

* * * * *

Revelation 2:12–15

The next letter was to the church at Pergamum, meaning "marriage." Also known as the compromising church, this church period extended from AD 313 to 590. The letter is as follows: "To the angel of the church in Pergamum write: These are the words of him who has the sharp, double-edged sword. I know where you live—where Satan has his throne. Yet you remain true to my name. You did not renounce your faith in me, not even in the days of Antipas, my faithful witness, who was put to death in your city—where Satan lives. Nevertheless, I have a few things against you: There are some among you who hold to the teaching of Balaam, who taught Balak to entice the Israelis to sin so that they ate food sacrificed to idols and committed sexual immorality. Likewise, you also have those who hold to the teaching of the Nicolaitans" (Revelation 2:12–15).

Satan's headquarters shifted from Babylon to Pergamum under the Romans. Pergamum became a very evil city with many pagan temples, including the especially evil temple of Aesculapius. Known as the Temple of the Snake, its followers offered sacrifices to Satan.

To relate this past church era to *how bad our modern world is becoming*, the Memphis paper, *The Commercial Appeal*, on December 21, 2014, had a story on its second page about how the Detroit chapter of the Satanic Temple had set up a "Snaketivity" scene on Michigan's capital lawn in Lansing. The scene included a snake offering a book titled *The Revolt of the Angels*. A nativity scene was then put up to counteract evil and represent "light and not darkness."

Pergamum had many people who believed in Balaam. History recorded that the Midianite women led the Israelite men into degenerate immoral acts. Jesus commends the people for keeping the faith under great distress.

Revelation 2:16

Revelation 2:16 instructs, "Repent therefore! Otherwise, I will soon come to you and will fight against them with the sword of my mouth." This expression, "with the sword of my mouth," may relate to God's awesome power, because God created everything in this universe, with the word of His mouth. Genesis 1 attests to the power of God's spoken word, because "God said." He spoke to create light, water, vegetation, fish, birds, and human beings. Consider also that even God's word in the written form (the Bible, which we also refer to as the Word) is very powerful; it is able to divide asunder, body and soul.

Revelation 2:17

Revelation 2:17 continues as follows: "Whoever has ears, let them hear what the Spirit says to the churches. To the one who is victorious, I will give some of the hidden manna. I will also give that person a white stone with a new name written on it, known only to the one who receives it." Jesus always used parables, expressing idioms or comparisons to the present day happenings of the Jewish people that his audience would be able to understand. The significance of the "white stone" is made clearer by Charles Ryrie. He wrote,

> The meaning of the white stone with a new name written is derived from either one or both of two customs of the day. The first was that judges who determined a verdict by placing in an urn a white and black pebble. If the white one came out, it meant acquittal; thus, the white stone would mean the assurance there is no condemnation to those who are in Christ Jesus. The other custom was the wearing of amulets, a good luck

charm worn around the neck. If this is the reference, then the stone is the Lord's way of reminding people that they had Him and needed no other King.[3]

In Pergamum, many Christians and Jews were martyred. Pergamum also had a library given to Cleopatra by Mark Antony. It contained over two hundred thousand writings, and parchment is believed to have been invented there. Most writings in those days were on papyrus or sheepskin. Pergamus was the city that Satan was using as his home base in John's day.

The Pergamum period extended from AD 313 to 590, and Constantine became emperor after the death of his father in AD 306. He became a believer in Christ Jesus and, in AD 313, wrote *Edict of Toleration*, which allowed everyone the right to choose his or her religion. Constantine built and started a church in Rome and gave gold pieces and white robes to all who joined his church and converted to Christianity. Constantine's zeal for the Lord caused many pagans, with their false beliefs, to join simply for the gold and robes.

Loraine Boettner listed the following *unscriptural* practices that came into the Roman church at this time: making prayers for the dead, making the sign of the cross, worshiping saints and angels, instituting the Mass, worshiping Mary, and establishing the doctrines of extreme unction and purgatory.[4] Of course, all of these practices remained when the Roman Church became the *Roman Catholic Church.*

The Roman emperor Theodosius (378–398) decided that Christianity would be the religion for the Roman Empire and made church membership and attendance compulsory. He also declared the *forcible suppression of any other religion* and forbade idol worship. These acts resulted in the Roman Empire's militarism forcefully coming into the church, bringing many heathen and unregenerate people. With Rome taking control, the church at Rome adopted the word *Catholic* in its title (an English translation of a Latin word meaning "universal"), because it believed itself to be the *only* church. The Roman Catholic Church wanted to be the prominent Christian, universal church. It became somewhat detached from Christ's church, and because of Rome's control, the worship service became a very imposing, elaborate ceremonial regimen, conducted with heathen, temple splendor. These actions led to the ministers of the service being called *priests*. All of this changed the church's spiritual image into one of Roman imperialism, giving it an apostate political design, which opened the door for a papal structure.

The Roman Church even *obliged itself* by imposing a bull, a fiat of the Roman Catholic Church, stating that *Rome and the Universe are one.*[5]

* * * * *

Revelation 2:18–23

Next comes John's letter to the church at Thyatira, meaning "continual sacrifice." This church period is illustrated by the Roman Catholic Church and lasted from AD 590 to 1517. The letter reads as follows:

> To the angel of the church in Thyatira write: These are the words of the Son of God, whose eyes are like blazing fire and whose feet are like burnished bronze. I know your deeds, your love and faith, your service and perseverance, and that you are now doing more than you did at first. Nevertheless, I have this against you: *You tolerate that woman Jezebel, who calls herself a prophet. By her teaching she misleads my servants into sexual immorality and the eating of food sacrificed to idols.* I have given her time to repent of her immorality, but she is unwilling. So I will cast her on a bed of suffering, and I will make those who commit adultery with her suffer intensely, unless they repent of her ways. I will strike her children dead. Then all the churches will know that I am he who searches hearts and minds, and I will repay each of you according to your deeds. (Revelation 2:18–23, emphasis added)

Apparently Jezebel was a prominent woman in the congregation. She taught sexual immorality and to eat food sacrificed to pagan idols. She was very unrepentant when warned. She was a believer in Antinomianism (liberalism), which had become very prevalent in the early church. This Jezebel reminds us of King Ahab's wife, the Jezebel mentioned in 1 Kings 16–19 and 2 Kings 9, who also was a murderous evil woman.

Revelation 2:24–25

Revelation 2:24–25 says, "Now I say to the rest of you in Thyatira, to you who do not hold to her teaching and have not learned Satan's so-called deep secrets, 'I will not impose any other burden on you, except to hold on to what you have until I come.'" To find out "Satan's so-called deep secrets," the Gnostics believed one had to join Satan's evil realm. Gnosticism stressed that knowing various ideas and concepts, as well as using ancient ideas from mythology, other religions, and even Christianity, would bring salvation.

In AD 500, church bishops began to apply the word *Father* to priests and bishops. Understand that there is only one father, Father God. In Matthew 23, Jesus warned the people about the Sadducees and Pharisees and how they prefer special places of honor at synagogues and meetings. Jesus told them, "But you are not to be called 'Rabbi,' for you have one Teacher, and you are all brothers. And do not call anyone on earth 'father,' for you have one Father, and he is in heaven" (8–9). However, many false practices continue even in today's churches.

As the Scriptures remind us, "Blessed is the one who trusts in the LORD, who does not look to the proud, to those who turn aside to false gods" (Psalm 40:4).

Revelation 2:26–29

Trusting Jesus brings many rewards, because He states: "To the one who is victorious and does my will to the end, I will give authority over the nations—that one 'will rule them with an iron scepter and will dash them to pieces like pottery'—just as I have received authority from my Father. I will also give that one the morning star. Whoever has ears, let them hear what the Spirit says to the churches" (Revelation 2:26–29).

* * * *

Revelation 3:1–3

The next church letter is to the church at Sardis, which means "remnant" and which is illustrated by the Reformation church. This church period extended from AD 1517 to 1700. Revelation 3:1–3 reads as follows:

> To the angel of the church in Sardis write: These are the words of him who holds the seven spirits of God and the seven stars. I know your deeds; you have a reputation of being alive, but you are dead. Wake up! Strengthen what remains and is about to die, for I have found your deeds unfinished in the sight of my God. Remember, therefore, what you have received and heard; hold it fast, and repent. But if you do not wake up, I will come like a thief, and you will not know at what time I will come to you. According to Pliny, the art of dying wool started in Sardis. Sardis was the center of colored dyed wool because of its location near Phrygia, with its large flocks of sheep. It was here that Turkish rugs first received beautiful colors. The hall, through which the king of Persia passed from his state apartments to the gate where he mounted his horse, had beautiful rugs. No one, but the monarch kings could walk on them.[6]

The Acropolis was in Sardis, but pictures show it was difficult to reach because of the terrain. This church period saw the start of the Reformation church, because of Martin Luther (1483–1546).

Revelation 3:4–6

Revelation 3:4–6 continues the letter to the church at Sardis as follows: "Yet you have a few people in Sardis who have not soiled their clothes. They will walk with me, dressed in white, for they are worthy. The one who is victorious will, like them, be dressed in white. I will never blot out the name of that person from the book of life, but will acknowledge that name before my Father and his angels. Whoever has ears, let them hear what the Spirit says to the churches."

The remains of the ancient city of Sardis are very few. The Gerusia, also called the house of Croesus, lies to the west of the acropolis. Arundel measured one of its halls and found it 156 feet in length by 43 feet in breadth; its walls were ten feet thick. Portions of a theater and of two churches were found, all of which consisted almost wholly of fragments of earlier edifices. One church, said to be dedicated to the Virgin, was carefully examined by Col. Leake, and from more recent investigations it appears that fragments were chiefly taken from the Temple of Cybele. If so, they are among the oldest monuments now existing in the world, the temple having been built only three hundred years after that of Solomon. Of the few inscriptions discovered, all or nearly all belong to the time of the Roman Empire. Yet there still exist considerable remains of the earlier days. The massive Temple of Cybele still bears witness, in its fragmentary remains, to the wealth and architectural skill of the people that raised it.[7]

* * * * *

Revelation 3:7–11

The next letter is to the church at Philadelphia, meaning "brotherly love." This church period is illustrated by the revival church period and extended from AD 1700 to 1900. The Bible tells us,

> To the angel of the church in Philadelphia write: These are the words of him who is holy and true, who holds the key of David. What he opens no one can shut, and what

he shuts no one can open. I know your deeds. See, I have placed before you an open door that no one can shut. I know that you have little strength, yet you have kept my word and have not denied my name. I will make those who are of the synagogue of Satan, who claim to be Jews though they are not, but are liars—I will make them come and fall down at your feet and acknowledge that I have loved you. Since you have kept my command to endure patiently, I will also keep you from the hour of trial that is going to come on the whole world to test the inhabitants of the earth. I am coming soon. Hold on to what you have, so that no one will take your crown. (Revelation 3:7–11)

Philadelphia is known as the city of brotherly love because Attilus II (220– 130 BC), who was one of the city's co-founders, gave the city to his brother, Eumenes II. It was an act of commemoration, love, and devotion to his brother. Philadelphia still exists as a Turkish town named Allah-Shehr, meaning "city of God." Philadelphia has soil that is rich, and fruits and vegetables are abundant. The river Cogamos abounds in fresh-water turtles, which are considered delicacies. The city depends on its corn, cotton, and tobacco crops, although the cotton grows in small pods. The town, poorly built and kept, is said to have exceedingly filthy streets. Six minarets, indicating as many mosques, are in the town.

This church historical period saw some of the great revivals in the United States. Jonathon Edwards (one of the United States' great preachers), John Wesley (the founder of the Methodist church), George Whitefield (a wonderful preacher and founder of the Presbyterian church), William Carey (a missionary to Burma), Adoniram Judson (a missionary to China), and many other evangelists of renown lived in this period.

Revelation 3:12–13

Revelation 3:12–13 says, "The one who is victorious I will make a pillar in the temple of my God. Never again will they leave it. I will write on them the name of my God and the name of the city of my

God, the new Jerusalem, which is coming down out of heaven from my God; and I will also write on them my new name. Whoever has ears, let them hear what the Spirit says to the churches."

Today's Christians of the church at Philadelphia, believe that one of the mosques was the church where the first Christians assembled. One solitary pillar of high antiquity has often been noted, reminding beholders of the remarkable words in the apocalyptic message to the Philadelphia church: "The one who is victorious I will make a pillar in the temple of my God." God Himself will make them *a pillar*. This may refer to those who are victorious over temptation and sin. Understand that a pillar is a foundational necessity to hold a building up. God will make that person very important in His heavenly realm and will mark that person as very special. Are you listening?

* * * * *

Revelation 3:14–19

The next letter is to *the church at Laodicea*, which means "people's rights." This church period, which extends from AD 1900 to the present, is illustrated by *the worldly church*. Revelation 3:14–19 says,

> To the angel of the church in Laodicea write: These are the words of the Amen, the faithful and true witness, the ruler of God's creation. I know your deeds, that you are neither cold nor hot. I wish you were either one or the other! So, because you are lukewarm—neither hot nor cold—I am about to spit you out of my mouth. You say, "I am rich; I have acquired wealth and do not need a thing." But you do not realize that you are wretched, pitiful, poor, blind and naked. I counsel you to buy from me gold refined in the fire, so you can become rich; and white clothes to wear, so you can cover your shameful nakedness; and salve to put on your eyes, so you can see. Those whom I love I rebuke and discipline. So be earnest and repent.

The statement, "I counsel you to buy from me gold refined in the fire, so you can become rich; and white clothes to wear, so you can cover your shameful nakedness; *and salve to put on your eyes*, so you can see," *may* relate to the greed of people. This city was noted for its wealth, banks, rich black apparel of wool, and eye salve. The garments created a textile cloth and rug-making business, and there was a medical school, which produced an eye salve named Tellurium. Antiochus II founded and named the Laodicea church after his wife, Laodicea.

Revelation 3:16 tells us, "So, because you are lukewarm—neither hot nor cold—I am about to spit you out of my mouth." As we have mentioned, Jesus used parables and idioms to reach people. They knew very well what He was talking about in His references to clothes, eye salve, and being "lukewarm." These verses illustrate the principle of parables, paradigms, and idioms that Jesus would use to teach his truths. Charles Ryrie explains Jesus use of *lukewarm* as follows: "Near Laodicea were hot mineral springs whose water could be drunk if very hot. When lukewarm, it was nauseating."[8]

Today, it is believed that we have become a lukewarm, worldly, liberal, self-seeking church, which leaves Jesus outside. In our world, only particular people, true believers and servants, are the ones who represent Jesus, and He will spew the liberal church out of His mouth.

Revelation 3:20–22

Revelation 3:20–22 says, "Here I am! I stand at the door and knock. If anyone hears my voice and opens the door, I will come in and eat with that person, and they with me. To the one who is victorious, I will give the right to sit with me on my throne, just as I was victorious and sat down with my Father on his throne. Whoever has ears, let them hear what the Spirit says to the churches." Jesus stands at the door. *Christ has done everything He can do to get people to listen and believe, without actually forcing them* to do so. Christ Jesus wants you to come of your own volition, that you would be happy with your decision. *The choice is yours.*

* * * * *

2

REVELATION 4:1–11:19

I declare to you, brothers and sisters, that *flesh and blood cannot inherit the kingdom of God*, nor does the perishable inherit the imperishable. Listen, I tell you a mystery: We will not all sleep, but we will all be changed—in a flash, in the twinkling of an eye, at the last trumpet. For the trumpet will sound, the dead will be raised imperishable, and we will be changed. *For the perishable must clothe itself with the imperishable, and the mortal with immortality.*

—1 Corinthians 15:50–53, emphasis added

Revelation 4:1

Revelation 4:1 signals a change of focus: "After this I looked, and there before me was *a door standing open in heaven*. And the voice I had first heard speaking to me like a trumpet said, *"Come up here, and I will show you what must take place after this"* (emphasis added). The first three chapters of Revelation refer to the "things which are," including the seven letters to the seven churches of John's day. Most theological scholars recognize the rapture occurring here in chapter 4, with "a door standing open in heaven." This word, *rapture*, is an English translation of a Latin word taken from the Latin Vulgate Bible. Its meaning is "caught up" or "caught out," but it has a root implication of "ecstasy in transport." I believe that fits our situation, for we will be *caught up* to meet the Lord in the air.

In 1 Thessalonians 4:16, the Bible teaches, *"For the Lord himself will come down from heaven*, with a loud command, with the voice of the archangel and *with the trumpet call of God, and the dead in Christ will rise first"* (emphasis added). The rapture will happen so that the true church, the believers in Christ as Savior, will not have to go through the great tribulation. God's wrath does not fall on His children.

The only God-fearing people left on earth after the rapture will be the Israelis and those who will convert when they realize the Bible was true. In any case, Satan will torment any who do not accept him, and he knows his time is short.

As previously stated, most biblical scholars believe that the "open door" that John saw refers to the rapture and that "what must take place after this" completes God's plans for Satan and humanity.

Revelation 4:2–6

In the next verses, John is taken to heaven's throne room, where he describes what he sees.

> At once *I was in the Spirit, and there before me was a throne in heaven with someone sitting on it*. And the one who sat there had the appearance of jasper and ruby. A rainbow that shone like an emerald encircled the throne. Surrounding the throne were twenty-four other thrones, and seated on them were twenty-four elders. They were dressed in white and had crowns of gold on their heads. From the throne came flashes of lightning, rumblings and peals of thunder. In front of the throne, seven lamps were blazing. *These are the seven spirits of God.* Also in front of the throne there was what looked like a sea of glass, clear as crystal. In the center, around the throne, were four living creatures, and they were covered with eyes, in front and in back. (Revelation 4:2–6, emphasis added)

John could not distinguish God, except to say, "The one who sat there had the appearance of jasper and ruby."

John did see and describe some of the angelic beings in this throne room whose primary purpose was to glorify and honor God. We too should laud, proclaim, praise, and worship His holy name—always. In Luke 10:27, Jesus explains what we are to do as God's creation: "He answered, '"Love the Lord your God with all your heart and with all your soul and with all your strength and with all your mind'; and, 'Love your neighbor as yourself.'"

Revelation 4:7–8

God now begins to tell us *the things that will occur after the rapture*: "The first living creature was like a lion, the second was like an ox, the third had a face like a man, the fourth was like a flying eagle. Each of the four living creatures had six wings and was covered with eyes all around, even under its wings. Day and night they never stop saying: '"Holy, holy, holy is the Lord God Almighty," who was, and is, and is to come" (Revelation 4:7–8). This expression, "who was, and is, and is to come"—or variations, such as, "These are the words of the First and Last, who died and came to life again"—is used many times in the book of Revelation. Perhaps God is trying to reinforce the fact that only God Himself in in control of all things.

These four living creatures around the throne must be very important, intelligent, and subservient to God. This is the very first mention in Revelation of creatures like these, which are different from cherubim and seraphim. However, perhaps the next few verses can help us understand more as we read of the vision given to Ezekiel: "Their faces looked like this: Each of the four had the face of a human being, and on the right side each had the face of a lion, and on the left the face of an ox; each also had the face of an eagle" (Ezekiel 1:10). The first living creature was like a lion. This reminds us of *Christ Jesus, the lion of the tribe of Judah*. The second creature was like an ox. Oxen are servants of human beings, and *Jesus came as to earth to be a servant for God*, as a perfect sacrifice for our sins. The third creature had the face of a man. *Jesus, the second person of the three in one, God Himself, was willing to become half-human*. The fourth creature was like a flying eagle. These four creatures appear to be symbolic of the blessed ministry of Christ in both the heavenly and earthly realms, because they never stop saying, "Holy, holy, holy is the Lord God Almighty, who was, and is, and is to come."

Revelation 4:9–11

Revelation 4:9–11 says, "Whenever the living creatures give glory, honor and thanks to him who sits on the throne and who lives for ever and ever, the twenty-four elders fall down before him who sits on the throne and worship him who lives for ever and ever. They lay their crowns before the throne and say: *"You are worthy, our Lord and God, to receive glory and honor and power, for you created all things, and by your will they were created and have their being"* (emphasis added). These thoughts describe worship. All living things—human beings, beasts, fish, and all plant life—should worship God, because He created everything from nothing. Only He—God—is able to do that, and *He alone deserves all worship.*

* * * * *

Revelation 5:1–5

The next verses say,

> Then I saw in the right hand of him who sat on the throne a scroll with writing on both sides and sealed with seven seals. And I saw a mighty angel proclaiming in a loud voice, *"Who is worthy to break the seals and open the scroll?"* But no one in heaven or on earth or under the earth could open the scroll or even look inside it. I wept and wept because no one was found who was worthy to open the scroll or look inside. Then one of the elders said to me, "Do not weep! See, *the Lion of the tribe of Judah, the Root of David, has triumphed. He is able to open the scroll and its seven seals"* (Revelation 5:1–5, emphasis added).

Only *God* is worthy enough to open the seven scrolls and seals. These seven scrolls foretell all that is about to happen. It is recorded that John wept because he thought no one could open the seals. His were the last tears in heaven, because Christ then comes forward and alleviates all sorrow.

Revelation 5:6

Revelation 5:6 says, "Then I saw a Lamb, looking as if it had been slain, standing at the center of the throne, encircled by the four living creatures and the elders. The Lamb had seven horns and seven eyes, which are the seven spirits of God sent out into all the earth." The "seven spirits of God" are defined for us in Revelation 4:5, where it tells us, "From the throne came flashes of lightning, rumblings and peals of thunder. In front of the throne, seven lamps were blazing. These are the *seven spirits of God*" (emphasis added). These "seven lamps blazing" are the seven spirits or seven churches Jesus sent into the world to proclaim the gospel.

Instead of John seeing a lion (verse 6), he sees a lamb that appears to be slain, but the lamb is our Lord, Jesus Christ. The Greek word used here for "slain" is *sphazo* (σφάζω), a word used to refer to a violent slaughter, which adequately describes Jesus as the crucified lamb.

The seven horns and seven eyes may refer to Christ's power in symbolic terms, because it is through His word, His Bible, and His churches that He proclaims *truth*.

John calls Jesus the lion of the tribe of Judah, the root of David. Jacob, in giving his blessing to his sons, said this about Judas's heritage: "You are a lion's cub, Judah; you return from the prey, my son. Like a lion he crouches and lies down, like a lioness—who dares to rouse him? *The scepter will not depart from Judah, nor the ruler's staff* from between his feet, until he to whom it belongs shall come and the obedience of the nations shall be his" (Genesis 49:9–10, emphasis added). The scepter and ruler's staff *belong to Christ Jesus*! Since David and Jesus were of the line of Judah, the scepter did not—nor will the ruler's staff—ever depart from Jesus, for He is the King of Kings and Lord of Lords.

Revelation 5:7–14

Revelation 5 continues as follows:

> He went and took the scroll from the right hand of him who sat on the throne. And when he had taken it, the four living creatures and the twenty-four elders fell down before the Lamb. Each one had a harp and they were holding golden bowls full of incense, which are the prayers of God's people. And they sang a new song, saying: "*You are worthy to take the scroll and to open its seals, because you were slain, and with your blood you purchased for God persons from every tribe and language and people and nation.* You have made them to be a kingdom and priests to serve our God, and they will reign on the earth." Then I looked and heard the voice of many angels, numbering thousands upon thousands, and ten thousand times ten thousand. They encircled the throne and the living creatures and the elders. In a loud voice they were saying: "*Worthy is the Lamb, who was slain, to receive power and wealth and wisdom and strength and honor and glory and praise!*" Then I heard every creature in heaven and on earth and under the earth and on the sea, and all that is in them, saying: "To him who sits on the throne and to the Lamb be praise and honor and glory and power, for ever and ever!" The four living creatures said, "Amen," and the elders fell down and worshiped. (Revelation 5:7–14, emphasis added)

John states that Jesus made those who have received Him as Lord "to be a kingdom and priests to serve our God, and they will reign on the earth" (Revelation 5:10). Those who have received Jesus as Savior will eventually reign on earth as priests in the kingdom of God. No one knows exactly what this means or all we will do, but eventually, when we are with the Lord, we will know. The angelic creatures worship, giving the Lord all honor, praise, and glory, which He deserves. Having been given free thought, they understand all that God has done for humanity. God has given you free thought. Do you understand?

*****

Revelation 6:1–2

Revelation 6:1–2 says, "I watched as the Lamb opened the first of the seven seals. Then I heard one of the four living creatures say in a voice like thunder, 'Come!' I looked, and there before me was a white horse! Its rider held a bow, and he was given a crown, and he rode out as a conqueror bent on conquest." The *seven-sealed scroll* contains the prophecy about the consequences that are to come to the world. These events will occur after the rapture of the Christian believers. God's wrath will begin the great tribulation.

As the Lamb opens the first seal, we see a white horse with a rider. This rider has a bow and a crown to go forth as a conqueror. There is some speculation about who this rider on a white horse is. Theologians register division. Some see this white horse and rider as Christ and His gospel come forth to conquer. Other scholars see this rider as a type of antichrist symbolizing the Roman Empire or church. This concept of the Roman Empire coming forth is easy to understand in connection with the ten Roman emperors. The ten emperors who persecuted Christ's church were Augustus Caesar, Tiberius, Nero, Galba, Otho, F. Vespasianus, Titus, Domitian, Nerva, and Trajan. Each of these wanted to conquer the world for Rome, but some were far more vicious in their maltreatment and persecution of Christians. A couple of these empire rulers literally slaughtered Christians.

This author considers the rider of the white horse to be symbolic of Satan's empire, simply because the other three horses and riders are part of God's wrath. With the Christians taken out between chapters three and four, the prophecy reveals that God's wrath will start to fall on the people left on earth. There *is* a description of Jesus on a white horse described *later*: "I saw heaven standing open and there *before me was a white horse, whose rider is called Faithful and True.* With justice he judges and wages war. His eyes are like blazing fire, and on his head are many crowns. *He has a name written on him that no one knows but he himself. He is dressed in a robe dipped in blood, and his name is the Word of God*" (Revelation 19:11–13, emphasis added). This is the true rider on the white horse, the Lord Jesus Himself!

Revelation 6:3–4

John, in chapters 4 and 5, was in heaven to reveal his vision. However, now, in chapter 6, the vision returns to earth after the rapture. We now begin to see the wrath of God start when Jesus opens the second seal: "When the Lamb opened the second seal, I heard the second living creature say, 'Come!' Then another horse came out, a fiery red one. Its rider was given power to take peace from the earth and to make people kill each other. To him was given a large sword" (Revelation 6:3–4).

Whatever peace was on the earth quickly vanishes after the rapture takes place. In shock, because of the sudden *disappearance of millions of people*, nation rises against nation to secure food, water, goods, and power in a chaotic world left without Christ's church. This fiery red horse symbolizes blood and death. Isaiah sums it up for us: "But the wicked are like the tossing sea, which cannot rest, whose waves cast up mire and mud. 'There is no peace,' says my God, 'for the wicked' (Isaiah 57:20–21).

Revelation 6:5–6

The next verses say, "When the Lamb opened the third seal, I heard the third living creature say, 'Come!' I looked, and there before me was a black horse! Its rider was holding a pair of scales in his hand. Then I heard what sounded like a voice among the four living creatures, saying, *'Two pounds of wheat for a day's wages, and six pounds of barley for a day's wages*, and do not damage the oil and the wine!'" (Revelation 6:5–6, emphasis added). The black horse is the catastrophe, famine, and death that will occur after the world suffers from lack of food and water. Food will be scarce, rationed, and very expensive. A day's wage will be required to buy two pounds of wheat or six pounds of barley. Even so, the very rich and powerful will not be too affected, because costly luxury items—oil and wine—will still be available.

Dr. Charles Ryrie writes that the third judgment brings famine to the world. The black horse forebodes death, and the pair of balances bespeaks a careful rationing of food. Normally, in Jesus's day, a "penny," a denarius, was a day's wages in Palestine. This amount of money would have bought eight measures of wheat and twenty-four of barley. In the prophecy, we see the same money only buying one-eighth of these goods. Only the rich will be able afford to buy food, so many people will starve to death.[1]

Revelation 6:7–8

Revelation 6:7–8 reads as follows: "When the Lamb opened the fourth seal, I heard the voice of the fourth living creature say, 'Come!' I looked, and there before me was a pale horse! Its rider was named Death, and Hades was following close behind him. They were given power over a fourth of the earth to kill by sword, famine and plague, and by the wild beasts of the earth." The rider of this fourth horse is named *Death*, and Hades follows close behind. This may refer to both the physical and spiritual application. Satan, in full command for a short time, will destroy multitudes of unbelievers left after the rapture. One fourth of the remaining people will die by plague, famine, or nations warring with each other. Death will also come by *wild beasts*. Not only will humanity be fighting for food, but also beasts will join in. Wild beasts here could easily include rats, vermin that contaminate with disease and plague. In any case, it will be a terrible time for humankind.

Revelation 6:9–11

Chapter six continues with the fifth seal: "When he opened the fifth seal, *I saw under the altar the souls of those who had been slain because of the word of God and the testimony they had maintained.* They called out in a loud voice, 'How long, Sovereign Lord, holy and true, until you judge the inhabitants of the earth and avenge our blood?' Then each of them was given a white robe, and they were told to wait a little longer, until the full number of their fellow servants, their brothers and sisters, were killed just as they had been" (Revelation 6:9–11, emphasis added). It seems apparent that these individuals under the altar had not received glorified spiritual bodies at the time of the rapture.

Some theological scholars suggest these are martyred believers, who, for the Word of God and belief in Jesus, died *after* the rapture. The Bible clearly indicates that all believers will be caught up, taken to heaven in the rapture. These prophesied individuals who are given white robes might be those who had defied Satan during the tribulation. These people did not receive Satan's mark and remained true to Christ to the point of martyrdom during the tribulation. There will people who will not believe in Jesus before the rapture but who will apparently understand and believe in Christ *after* the rapture occurs. However, they are to be martyred for Jesus and the gospel's sake.

The following verses describe for us what the martyred ones gained in refusing to accept Satan's image and mark.

> A third angel followed them and said in a loud voice: "*If anyone worships the beast and its image and receives its mark on their forehead or on their hand, they, too, will drink the wine of God's fury, which has been poured full strength into the cup of his wrath.* They will be tormented with burning sulfur in the presence of the holy angels and of the Lamb. And the smoke of their torment will rise for ever and ever. There will be no rest day or night for those who worship the beast and its image, or for anyone who receives the mark of its name." This calls for patient endurance on the part of the people of God who keep his commands and remain faithful to Jesus. Then I heard a voice from heaven say, "Write this: Blessed are the dead who die in the Lord from now on." "Yes," says the Spirit, "they will rest from their labor, for their deeds will follow them." (Revelation 14:9–13, emphasis added)

Those who choose the antichrist will suffer greatly. Some have concluded that the antichrist will come from the tribe of Dan, based on Genesis 49:17, which says, "Dan will be a snake by the roadside, a viper along the path, that bites the horse's heels so that its rider tumbles backward." Theologians also use Jeremiah 8:16 to inform us concerning this matter: "The snorting of the enemy's horses is heard from Dan; at the neighing of their stallions the whole land trembles. They have come to devour the land and everything in it, the city and all who live there."

Revelation 6:12–17

Next comes the sixth seal.

> I watched as he opened the sixth seal. There was a great earthquake. The sun turned black like sackcloth made of goat hair, *the whole moon turned blood red*, and the stars in the sky fell to earth, as figs drop from a fig tree when shaken by a strong wind. The heavens receded like a scroll being rolled up, *and every mountain and island was removed from its place*. Then the kings of the earth, the princes, the generals, the rich, the mighty, and everyone else, both slave and free, hid in caves and among the rocks of the mountains. They called to the mountains and the rocks, *"Fall on us and hide us from the face of him who sits on the throne and from the wrath of the Lamb! For the great day of their wrath has come, and who can withstand it?"* (Revelation 6:12–17, emphasis added)

Once again, there is some debate about the timing of the events spoken of in verses 6:12–17. *Some* expositors and theologians believe these events happened with the fall of Jerusalem and the evil time following, with literally murderous Roman emperors like Trajan in control. That thought does not seem to fit, because Jesus told John, *"After this* I looked, and there before me was a door standing open in heaven. And the voice I had first heard speaking to me like a trumpet said, "Come up here, and I will show you what must take place after this" (Revelation 4:1, emphasis added). As was intimated, the "after this" is the rapture, so the events described by verses 12 through 17 could not have happened before the rapture.

In addition, with all the destruction going on, stubborn, unrepentant people cry for the mountains and rocks to fall on them instead of crying for mercy and forgiveness of sins. Isaiah had a vision of enemies attacking Jerusalem. This visualization (Revelation 6:12–17) could also easily illustrate the time spoken of by Isaiah.

Woe to you, Ariel, Ariel, the city where David settled! Add year to year and let your cycle of festivals go on. Yet I will besiege Ariel; she will mourn and lament, she will be to me like an altar hearth. I will encamp against you on all sides; I will encircle you with towers and set up my siege works against you. Brought low, you will speak from the ground; your speech will mumble whisper. But your many enemies will become like fine dust, the ruthless hordes like blown chaff. Suddenly, in an instant. The LORD Almighty will come with thunder and earthquake and great noise, with windstorm and tempest and flames of a devouring fire. Then the hordes of all the nations that fight against Ariel, that attack her and her fortress and besiege her, will be as it is with a dream, with a vision in the night— (Isaiah 29:1–7)

Ariel is the symbolic name of Jerusalem and a symbolic term for an Israelite. The Hebrew word *ariel* translates as "lion of God" or "lion like." McClintock and Strong tell us that this word, when applied to Jerusalem, translates symbolically "as victorious under God."[2] The implication of "Ariel," is that God will always defend and win against Satan, regardless of the circumstance or place, and that this is especially concerning God's chosen people and city, Jerusalem.

Even if Isiah's mental imagery does apply to sometime before the tribulation, this forecast could also easily apply to the Revelation event (John's vision). Isaiah may have then depicted the last attack on Jerusalem with the battle of Armageddon. Moreover, my guess is that what is shown here seems to be God's wrath coming to the nations who have besieged Israel as well as to those who will besiege Israel at Armageddon. Earlier, Isaiah says, "Woe to the wicked! Disaster is upon them! They will be paid back for what their hands have done" (Isaiah 3:11).

* * * * *

Revelation 7:1–8

Revelation 7 gives us twelve thousand servants of God from each tribe mentioned. There are twelve thousand from the tribes of Judah, Reuben, Gad, Asher, Naphtali, Manasseh, Simeon, Levi, Issachar, Zebulon, Joseph, and Benjamin. Here are the first eight verses:

> After this I saw four angels standing at the four corners of the earth, holding back the four winds of the earth to prevent any wind from blowing on the land or on the sea or on any tree. Then I saw another angel coming up from the east, having the seal of the living God. He called out in a loud voice to the four angels who had been given power to harm the land and the sea: "Do not harm the land or the sea or the trees until we put a seal on the foreheads of the servants of our God." Then I heard the number of those who were sealed: 144,000 from all the tribes of Israel. From the tribe of Judah 12,000 were sealed, from the tribe of Reuben 12,000, from the tribe of Gad 12,000, from the tribe of Asher 12,000, from the tribe of Naphtali 12,000, from the tribe of Manasseh 12,000, from the tribe of Simeon 12,000, from the tribe of Levi 12,000, from the tribe of Issachar 12,000, from the tribe of Zebulun 12,000, from the tribe of Joseph 12,000, from the tribe of Benjamin 12,000. (Revelation 7:1–8)

Note that Judah heads up the list and not Reuben, the firstborn. Also note that both Dan and Ephraim are missing. Both tribes were guilty of going into idolatry (Judges 18, 1 Kings 11, Hosea 4). The tribes of Levi and Manasseh take Dan and Ephraim's place. However, both tribes are listed in Ezekiel's millennial temple, shown in Ezekiel 48.

Apparently, there is a short break to link the events of God's wrath between the sixth and seventh judgments. He describes two significant happenings. First, the four angels have power over the land, sea, and trees, and they are not allowed to do further harm until the 144,000 are sealed. We then see the calling of 144,000 Jews, 12,000 from each tribe mentioned. These called ones appear to be either evangelists or special Hebrew servants for God who will bring people to Him during the tribulation period. My reasons for saying this will better understood in the next verses, where multitudes of saved individuals are before the throne of God.

Again, twelve thousand will be chosen from each tribe, sealed as special servants of God. I'm sure their mission during this terrible tribulation will not be easy with Satan so prominent and committed to killing all Jews and Christians. However, God's will, and His will alone, will be done. He will give them power to accomplish His task, whatever it may be.

Revelation 7:9–12

Following are the next verses in chapter 7:

> After this I looked, and there before me was a great multitude that no one could count, from every nation, tribe, people and language, standing before the throne and before the Lamb. They were wearing white robes and were holding palm branches in their hands. And they cried out in a loud voice: "*Salvation belongs to our God, who sits on the throne, and to the Lamb.*" All the angels were standing around the throne and around the elders and the four living creatures. They fell down on their faces before the throne and worshiped God, saying: "*Amen! Praise and glory and wisdom and thanks and honor and power and strength be to our God for ever and ever. Amen!*" (Revelation 7:9–12, emphasis added).

Even during the "great" tribulation persecutions, God will save many.

Revelation 7:13–17

The following verses show us these saved individuals wearing the white robes of righteousness before the throne of God:

Then one of the elders asked me, "These in white robes—who are they, and where did they come from?" I answered, "Sir, you know." And he said, *"These are they who have come out of the great tribulation; they have washed their robes and made them white in the blood of the Lamb.* Therefore, "they are before the throne of God and serve him day and night in his temple; and he who sits on the throne will shelter them with his presence. *'Never again* will they hunger; *never again* will they thirst. The sun will not beat down on them,' nor any scorching heat. For the Lamb at the center of the throne will be their shepherd; 'he will lead them to springs of living water.' 'And God will wipe away every tear from their eyes.'" (Revelation 7:13–17, emphasis added)

Again, we see the "multitude" as being those who have come out of the great tribulation; they have washed their robes and made them white in the blood of the Lamb.

* * * * *

Revelation 8:1–5

In chapter 8, the seventh seal is broken.

When he opened the seventh seal, there was silence in heaven for about half an hour. And I saw the seven angels who stand before God, and seven trumpets were given to them. Another angel, who had a golden censer, came and stood at the altar. He was given much incense to offer, with the prayers of all God's people, on the golden altar in front of the throne. The smoke of the incense, together with the prayers of God's people, went up before God from the angel's hand. Then the angel took the censer, filled it with fire from the altar, and hurled it on the earth; and there came peals of thunder, rumblings, flashes of lightning and an earthquake. (Revelation 8:1– 5, emphasis added)

When the seventh and last seal is broken, *silence will reign in heaven for thirty minutes* before the seven trumpets sound. The number thirty, in this case, seems to denote mourning or sorrow. This silence may be one of expectation, just thinking about the dreadful time that is about to come upon the people left on the earth. Perhaps the silence is God giving humanity one more chance to think and receive Him as Lord. As the Bible says elsewhere, "Be still before the LORD, all mankind, because he has roused himself from his holy dwelling" (Zechariah 2:13).

Some expositors believe that the angel taking the censer is Jesus hurling the fire of the altar to earth. However, Jesus *is the Son of God*, so being called an angel does not seem to fit.

The verses mention the "prayers of God's people." This will be a time of great stress, so God's people will need to pray, for no one else will. Perhaps these prayers will ask for justice and righteousness to God for many the evils that transpired before the rapture. All we know is that God will be avenging Himself. People will not have listened and will have chosen their own way, totally leaving God out. In Ezekiel 33:11, God describes His feelings concerning this matter: "Say to them, 'As surely as I live, declares the Sovereign LORD, I take no pleasure in the death of the wicked, but rather that they turn from their ways and live. Turn! Turn from your evil ways! Why will you die, people of Israel?'"

Revelation 8:6–7

The next verses are as follows: "Then the seven angels who had the seven trumpets prepared to sound them. The first angel sounded his trumpet, *and there came hail and fire mixed with blood*, and it was hurled down on the earth. *A third of the earth was burned up, a third of the trees were burned up, and all the green grass was burned* up" (Revelation 8:6–7, emphasis added). The result of the angel throwing the fire from the altar produces "hail and fire mixed with blood" falling on the earth, plus peals of thunder, rumblings, flashes of lightning, and an earthquake. Hail can be very damaging, but it is even more frightening with blood mixed in. With a third of all vegetation, trees, plants, and grass burned up, breathing could become a problem due to the lack of oxygen. All of this is just a harbinger of what is to come next in the prophecy, as the seven angels with the seven trumpets are about to release their woes.

Revelation 8:8–9

Revelation 8:8–9 tells us, "The second angel sounded his trumpet, and *something like a huge mountain, all ablaze, was thrown into the sea. A third of the sea turned into blood, a third of the living creatures in the sea died, and a third of the ships were destroyed*" (emphasis added). This could easily refer to a comet or some kind of asteroid space debris striking the earth. Science well knows earth is assaulted regularly with comets and chunks of planets, but humankind has been fortunate up to this point, in that none of them were large enough to do much damage. However, when God begins to punish the unbelievers, things will get very dicey.

A *third* of the sea will turn to blood, killing a *third* of all creatures living in the oceans. Having a *third* of all ships destroyed would be a terrible blow to the transporting of goods, food, and supplies. The human beings left on earth will be getting desperate.

Revelation 8:10–11

Revelation 8:10–11says, "The third angel sounded his trumpet, and *a great star, blazing like a torch, fell from the sky on a third of the rivers and on the springs of water—the name of the star is Wormwood*. A third of the waters turned bitter, and many people died from the waters that had become bitter" (emphasis added). The third angel brings events similar to the second angel's blown trumpet. Again, a large blazing star, comet, or asteroid chunk falls on rivers and springs to turn drinking water bitter, so that it is poisoned. The last verse tells us that human beings will then have less food and water and fewer transporting ships.

Things will get tougher as the great tribulation moves along.

Revelation 8:12

Revelation 8:12 reads as follows: "The fourth angel sounded his trumpet, and *a third of the sun* was struck, *a third of the moon*, and *a third of the stars, so that a third of them turned dark. A third of the day was without light, and also a third of the night*" (emphasis added). Once again, we see one-third being the prominent number. The number three in Scripture is *usually* a heavenly *God-directed number.* He is the great three-in-one. Jesus was tempted three times. Jesus rose from the dead on the third day. The list of godly threes goes on. In addition, we now see one-third of the day and the night taken away in this prophecy. Without light, things get scarier, and without sunlight, nothing grows. Living in darkness is not pleasant. As this verse illustrates, God will make the night shorter so that there will be no rest for the people remaining on earth.

Revelation 8:13

In Revelation 8:13, we read what comes next: "As I watched, I heard an eagle that was flying in midair call out in a loud voice: '*Woe! Woe! Woe to the inhabitants of the earth*, because of the trumpet blasts about to be sounded by the other three angels!'" (emphasis added). Biblical scholars believe that with the three repetitions of *woe*, the *worst part* of the great tribulation will start to happen. With all that will have come about thus far, it would seem *unreasonable* to say that the worst is yet to come, but apparently it is the case.

* * * * *

Revelation 9:1–5

In the next chapter, we read about the next trumpet blast.

> The fifth angel sounded his trumpet, and *I saw a star that had fallen from the sky to the earth.* The star was given the key to the shaft of the Abyss. When he opened

the Abyss, smoke rose from it like the smoke from a gigantic furnace. *The sun and sky were darkened by the smoke from the Abyss.* And out of the smoke *locusts came down on the earth and were given power like that of scorpions* of the earth. They were told not to harm the grass of the earth or any plant or tree, but only those people who did not have the seal of God on their foreheads. *They were not allowed to kill them but only to torture them for five months.* And the agony they suffered was like that of the sting of a scorpion when it strikes. (Revelation 9:1–5)

The word *abyss* in the original Greek means "bottomless pit." Apparently, Satan will get the key to the Abyss so that he can release his fellow demons. This bottomless pit is mentioned *seven* times in the book of Revelation, and each incident is in relation to demons and fallen angels held for judgment. Recall that Satan tried to take over from God, and many experts believe "the fallen star" in the verses above is Satan. Jesus has control of, and the key to, the Abyss, as told in *Luke:* "And they begged Jesus repeatedly not to order them to go into the Abyss" (8:31).

Isaiah tells us a little more about Satan.

All your pomp has been brought down to the grave, along with the noise of your harps; maggots are spread out beneath you and worms cover you. *How you have fallen from heaven, morning star, son of the dawn! You have been cast down to the earth,* you who once laid low the nations! *You said in your heart, "I will* ascend to the heavens; *I will* raise my throne above the stars of God; *I will* sit enthroned on the mount of assembly, on the utmost heights of Mount Zaphon. *I will* ascend above the tops of the clouds; *I will* make myself like the Most High." (Isaiah 14:12–14, emphasis added)

God cast Satan from heaven, along with many angels who sided with him. Angels, like human beings, have free will to choose. The Bible informs us that one-third of angels in heaven decided to go with

Satan. Satan talked those angels into abandoning God, and most of them were locked up until the day of judgment.

However, in Revelation 9:1–5, we read that Satan will release some of them. It is ironic justice, but *God uses His enemies to persecute His enemies*: "And the angels who did not keep their positions of authority but abandoned their proper dwelling—these he has kept in darkness, bound with everlasting chains for judgment on the great Day" (Jude 1:6). Some demon angels remained with Satan while he was prince of the air. Apparently, that was done so that they could persecute humankind until Christ's return. However, in the end, all demon angels end up in the lake of fire.

Nonetheless, in the tribulation, Satan will be able to release his demon multitude upon the earth. Ironically, as we mentioned, *God uses Satan* and his followers *to punish those who follow Satan and refuse to believe in the Lord God*.

Revelation 9:6

Revelation 9:6 says, "During those days people will seek death but will not find it; they will long to die, but death will elude them." These demon scorpions are so fierce that *people want to commit suicide*, actually kill themselves, *to be relieved of the pain and torment*. Nevertheless, no human will be able to die during this period. According to a footnote for this verse in Zondervan's *NIV Study Bible*, Cornelius Gallus, a Roman poet of the first century, wrote, "Worse than any wound is the wish to die, and yet not be able to do so."

Revelation 9:7–10

Next, Revelation 9:7–10 says, "The locusts looked like horses prepared for battle. On their heads they wore something like crowns of gold, and their faces resembled human faces. Their hair was like women's hair, and their teeth were like lions' teeth. They had breastplates like breastplates of iron, and the sound of their wings was like the thundering of many horses and chariots rushing into battle. They had tails with stingers, like scorpions, and in their tails they had power to torment people for five months." John's description of the released locusts presents fierce critters designed to inflict pain and suffering. Their scorpion-like sting is very painful. They will not be allowed to hurt God's marked ones, but their reign will last for five months of torture and agony for unbelievers. Five months is the normal life cycle of locusts.

Revelation 9:11

Revelation 9:11 tells us, "They had as king over them the angel of the Abyss, whose name in Hebrew is Abaddon and in Greek is Apollyon (that is, Destroyer)." Satan is not only evil in opposing God, but he is also the great imitator of God. God has Christ, and Satan has his antichrist. The word antichrist does not appear in the book of Revelation. In fact, it only appears five times in the Bible, in the following four verses:

Dear children, this is the last hour; and as you have heard that the antichrist is coming, even now many *antichrists* have come. This is how we know it is the last hour. (1 John 2:18, emphasis added)

Who is a liar but he that denieth that Jesus is the Christ? He is *antichrist*, that denieth the Father and the Son. (1 John 2:22, emphasis added)

[B]ut every spirit that does not acknowledge Jesus is not from God. This is the spirit of the *antichrist*, which you have heard is coming and even now is already in the world. (1 John 4:3, emphasis added)

I say this because many deceivers, who do not acknowledge Jesus Christ as coming in the flesh, have gone out into the world. Any such person is the deceiver and the *antichrist*. (2 John 1:7, emphasis added)

The impression in Revelation 9:11 is that the demon angels have a king over them, but Satan is really in charge. On that premise, apparently Abaddon or Apollyon is a type of satanic anti-archangel, perhaps an imitation of Michael, God's archangel.

Revelation 9:12–17

Chapter 9 continues as follows:

> *The first woe is past; two other woes are yet to come.* The sixth angel sounded his trumpet, and I heard a voice coming from the four horns of the golden altar that is before God. It said to the sixth angel who had the trumpet, "Release the four angels who are bound at the great river Euphrates." And the four angels who had been kept ready for this very hour and day and month and year were released to kill a third of mankind. The number of the mounted troops was twice ten thousand times ten thousand. I heard their number. The horses and riders I saw in my vision looked like this: Their breastplates were fiery red, dark blue, and yellow as sulfur. The heads of the horses resembled the heads of lions, and out of their mouths came fire, smoke and sulfur. (Revelation 9:12–17, emphasis added)

Two hundred million mounted troops, on special fire-breathing horses, will kill *one-third* of humankind. Again, apparently these demons will be in reserve, ready for this very job of killing one-third of the unbelievers left on earth. *If you do not know Christ as savior, you could possibly be one of these left to face God's wrath. Think about it!*

Revelation 9:18–21

Here is what comes next:

> A third of mankind was killed by the three plagues of fire, smoke and sulfur that came out of their mouths. The power of the horses was in their mouths and in their tails; for their tails were like snakes, having heads with which they inflict injury. *The rest of mankind who were not killed by these plagues still did not repent of the work of their hands; they did not stop worshiping demons, and*

> *idols of gold, silver, bronze, stone and wood—idols that cannot see or hear or walk.* Nor did they repent of their murders, their magic arts, their sexual immorality or their thefts. (Revelation 9:18–21, emphasis added)

At this point, over one-half of the world's population will be gone, so what does humankind do? Human beings try magic or cultism to protect themselves. *With all that will be going on, the people who left will not repent or even acknowledge God.*

People, even under great duress and suffering, will still *not want to acknowledge* God and will not pay any attention to Him. They will continue to choose oblivion.

* * * * *

Revelation 10:1–4

Chapter 10 opens with the following vision:

> Then I saw another mighty angel coming down from heaven. He was robed in a cloud, with a rainbow above his head; his face was like the sun, and his legs were like fiery pillars. He was holding a little scroll, which lay open in his hand. He planted his right foot on the sea and his left foot on the land, and he gave a loud shout like the roar of a lion. When he shouted, the voices of the seven thunders spoke. And when the seven thunders spoke, I was about to write; but I heard a voice from heaven say, *"Seal up what the seven thunders have said and do not write it down."* (Revelation 10:1–4, emphasis added)

This vision depicts a mighty angel coming down from heaven to do God's work, as directed. This may not be Jesus, because verse 6 says: "And he swore by him who lives for ever and ever, who created the heavens and all that is in them, the earth and all that is in it, and the sea and all that is in it" (Revelation 10:6). Some commentators believe this angel might be the archangel Michael.

We noted an apparent time interval between the sixth and seventh seal's opening, and now another interlude appears between the sixth and seventh trumpets. Whatever the seven thunders will say is not written; it is sealed.

Revelation 10:5–7

Revelation 10:5–7 says, "Then the angel I had seen standing on the sea and on the land raised his right hand to heaven. And *he swore by him who lives for ever and ever*, who created the heavens and all that is in them, the earth and all that is in it, and the sea and all that is in it, and said, 'There will be no more delay! But in the days when the seventh angel is about to sound his trumpet, the mystery of God will be accomplished, just as he announced to his servants the prophets'" (emphasis added). This powerful angel announces that there will be no more delay before God's wrath will be poured out in what will be the last three-and-one-half years of the great tribulation. Three-and-one-half years can be a *very long time* when one is suffering the wrath of God.

Revelation 10:8–11

Revelation 10:8–11 reports what happens next.

> Then the voice that I had heard from heaven spoke to me once more: "Go, take the scroll that lies open in the hand of the angel who is standing on the sea and on the land." So I went to the angel and asked him to give me the little scroll. He said to me, "Take it and eat it. It will turn your stomach sour, but 'in your mouth it will be as sweet as honey.'" I took the little scroll from the angel's hand and ate it. It tasted as sweet as honey in my mouth, but when I had eaten it, my stomach turned sour. Then I was told, "You must prophesy again about many peoples, nations, languages and kings."

John is told to eat the scroll, and *Willmington's Guide to the Bible* gives us one explanation. Up to this point, John has seen the first part of the tribulation, and it has been sweet indeed to witness ungodly people receiving their just punishment. At this point, he will preview the last three-and-one- half years of the tribulation. This period will begin with the wholesale slaughter of Israel's people by the antichrist. This was indeed bitter medicine to John.

* * * * *

Revelation 11:1–2

Revelation 11:1–2 says, "I was given a reed like a measuring rod and was told, 'Go and measure the temple of God and the altar, with its worshipers. But exclude the outer court; do not measure it, because it has been given to the Gentiles. They will trample on the holy city for 42 months.'" This verse announces the last three-and-one-half year period (forty-two months) that Satan and his minions will be able to persecute and abuse the Jews and any believers who have converted to Christianity. John measures and records the true temple size in heaven, with its worshipers of God, but excludes the outer court of the Gentiles.

Jesus predicted this future for His disciples when they asked Him when these things would happen and for a sign of the times: "They will fall by the sword and will be taken as prisoners to all the nations. Jerusalem will be trampled on by the Gentiles until the times of the Gentiles are fulfilled" (Luke 21:24). The forty-two month period is mentioned in Daniel: "He will speak against the Most High and oppress his holy people and try to change the set times and the laws. *The holy people will be delivered into his hands for a time, times and half a time*" (Daniel 7:25, emphasis added). The phrase "for a time, times and half a time" means three-and-one-half years. A "time," according to theologians, is considered to be one year. Daniel's prophecy helps us understand the tribulation period.

Daniel mentions this time-period again: "The man clothed in linen, who was above the waters of the river, lifted his right hand and his left hand toward heaven, and I heard him swear by him who lives forever, saying, 'It will be for a time, times and half a time. When the power of the holy people has been finally broken, all these things will be completed'" (Daniel 12:7).

Revelation 11:3–8

Next we will see *two witnesses* come onto the scene, and how the world will react and treat these spokespersons for God. Jesus has said, "The world cannot hate you, but it hates me because I testify that its works are evil" (John 7:7).

> "And I will appoint my two witnesses, and they will prophesy for 1,260 days, clothed in sackcloth." They are "the two olive trees" and the two lampstands, and "they stand before the Lord of the earth." If anyone tries to harm them, fire comes from their mouths and devours their enemies. This is how anyone who wants to harm them must die. They have power to shut up the heavens so that it will not rain during the time they are prophesying; and they have power to turn the waters into blood and to strike the earth with every kind of plague as often as they want. Now when they have finished their testimony, the beast that comes up from the Abyss will attack them, and overpower and kill them. *Their bodies will lie in the public square of the great city—which is figuratively called Sodom and Egypt—where also their Lord was crucified.* (Revelation 11:3–8, emphasis added)

Jerusalem will become so sinful and evil that it will be "spiritually called Sodom and Egypt." These terms are used because of Sodom's immorality and Egypt's being so worldly. Jerusalem, God's city, will become so evil and corrupt that it will become part of the world instead of being distinct as God's city.

Satan's beast from the Abyss will not be able to kill the two witnesses until they finish their testimony. It is not known who these two witnesses will be, but speculation leads to Elijah and Enoch, because they did not see death. Hebrews 9:27 states, "Just as people are *destined to die once, and after that to face judgment*" (emphasis added). As Genesis 5:19–24 explains, Enoch and Elijah were taken to heaven without seeing mortal death: "After he became the father of Enoch, Jared lived 800 years and had other sons and daughters. Altogether, Jared lived a total of 962 years, and then he died. When Enoch had lived 65 years, he became the father of Methuselah. After he became the father of Methuselah, Enoch walked faithfully with God 300 years and had other sons and daughters. Altogether, Enoch lived a total of 365 years. Enoch walked faithfully with God; then he was no more, because God took him away."

This is also described in 2 Kings 2:9–11, as follows: "When they had crossed, Elijah said to Elisha, 'Tell me, what can I do for you before I am taken from you?' 'Let me inherit a double portion of your spirit,' Elisha replied. 'You have asked a difficult thing,' Elijah said, 'yet if you see me when I am taken from you, it will be yours—otherwise, it will not.' As they were walking along and talking together, suddenly a chariot of fire and horses of fire appeared and separated the two of them, and Elijah went up to heaven in a whirlwind."

Although Elijah and Enoch had been taken to heaven in a type of rapture, these verses from Revelation suggest that they *may possibly* have to face *physical death* as martyrs for God.

Other theologians hold that the two witnesses could be Elijah and Moses, because they came back to talk to Jesus in front of the disciples. Note the following Scriptures:

> See, I will send the prophet Elijah to you before that great and dreadful day of the LORD comes. He will turn the hearts of the parents to their children, and the hearts of the children to their parents; or else I will come and strike the land with total destruction. (Malachi 4:5–6)

> After six days Jesus took with him Peter, James and John the brother of James, and led them up a high mountain by themselves. There he was transfigured before them. His face shone like the sun, and his clothes became as white as the light. Just then there appeared before them Moses and Elijah, talking with Jesus. (Matthew 17:1–3)

Another thought to consider about Moses being one of the witnesses comes to us from Jude 9: "But even the *archangel Michael*, when he was *disputing* with the devil about the body of Moses, did not himself dare to condemn him for slander but said, 'The Lord rebuke you!'" (emphasis added). The idea here is that perhaps Satan wanted to acquire Moses's body so that he could not be one of God's witnesses against the antichrist during the tribulation. Speculation says that God may bring Moses back to life as a witness.

Revelation 11:9–12

Revelation 11 continues,

> *For three and a half days some from every people, tribe, language and nation will gaze on their bodies and refuse them burial.* The inhabitants of the earth will gloat over them and will celebrate by sending each other gifts, because these two prophets had tormented those who live on the earth. *But after the three and a half days the breath of life from God entered them*, and they stood on their feet, and terror struck those who saw them. Then they heard a loud voice from heaven saying to them, "Come up here." *And they went up to heaven in a cloud, while their enemies looked on.* (Revelation 11:9– 12, emphasis added)

It is easy to imagine TV or the Internet (possibly both) being used here. Perhaps that is why this book remained unopened before. When they did not have TV or the Internet, how could people from the whole world see the bodies of Gods witnesses in three and one-half days

The people left on earth celebrate the death of the two witnesses, believing they have gained some sort of victory. However, their joy is short-lived, as God breathes life back into His witnesses. Can you imagine the terror of seeing a dead body of three and one-half days rise to its feet? Do not be one of those left behind! Simply accept Jesus as Lord and Savior.

Revelation 11:13–19

Revelation 11:13–19 reads as follows:

> At that very hour there was a severe earthquake and a tenth of the city collapsed. Seven thousand people were killed in the earthquake, and the survivors were terrified and gave glory to the God of heaven. The second woe has passed; the third woe is coming soon. The seventh angel sounded his trumpet, and there were loud voices in heaven, which said: "The kingdom of the world has become the kingdom of our Lord and of his Messiah, and he will reign for ever and ever." And the twenty-four elders, who were seated on their thrones before God, fell on their faces and worshiped God, saying: "We give thanks to you, Lord God Almighty, the One who is and who was, because you have taken your great power and have begun to reign. The nations were angry, and your wrath has come. The time has come for judging the dead, and for rewarding your servants the prophets and your people who revere your name, both great and small—and for destroying those who destroy the earth." Then God's temple in heaven was opened, and within his temple was seen the ark of his covenant. And there came flashes of lightning, rumblings, peals of thunder, an earthquake and a severe hailstorm.

With the two witnesses coming back to life, these verses prophesy that an earthquake will level one-tenth of the city. Some terrified survivors will then begin to give glory to God. Two "woes" will have occurred, and the third and final woe will soon happen.

With the seventh angel's trumpet announcement, these verses describe the twenty-four elders worshiping and glorifying God. The temple in heaven opens, and the *ark of the covenant* is seen once more. When this happens, the ark of the covenant will not have been seen for thousands of years. One reason for this is given by Jeremiah: "And it shall come to pass, when ye be multiplied and increased in the land, in those days, saith the LORD, they shall say no more, *The ark of the covenant of the LORD: neither shall it come to mind: neither shall they remember it; neither shall they visit it; neither shall that be done any more"* (Jeremiah 3:16, emphasis added). Indeed, most people do not even think about the ark of the covenant or Noah's ark, because they barely, if ever, think about God. One example of humankind not thinking about God is illustrated by the fact that Noah's ark remains on Mount Ararat in Turkey. Historical verification has shown it to be there, but no one is interested in believing confirmation of God's wondrous book, the Bible.

God took His ark of the covenant to heaven to keep it safe from sinful people. Be very grateful that God thinks about and does not forget you!

* * * * *

3

REVELATION 12:1–13:18

> The wrath of God is being revealed from heaven against all the godlessness and wickedness of people, who suppress the truth by their wickedness …
>
> —Romans 1:18

Revelation 12 and 13 give us a respite, with a short review of things past that led up to the present and to the great tribulation. As we continue, God shows us Satan, with his God-given power, during the tribulation period.

Revelation 12:1–4

Chapter 12 begins as follows:

> *A great sign appeared in heaven*: a woman clothed with the sun, with the moon under her feet and a crown of twelve stars on her head. She was pregnant and cried out in pain as she was about to give birth. *Then another sign appeared in heaven: an enormous red dragon with seven heads and ten horns and seven crowns on its heads.* Its tail swept a third of the stars out of the sky and flung them to the earth. *The dragon stood in front of the woman who was about to give birth, so that it might devour her child the moment he was born.* (Revelation 12:1–4, emphasis added)

Most expositors of the Bible see this "great wonder" of the pregnant woman with the "crown of twelve stars" as representing the Hebrew nation giving birth to Jesus and the birth of the church through Christ. The church came from the original Hebrew nation represented by the "twelve stars" and the twelve apostles. This woman is described as being "clothed with the sun," which clearly corresponds to Jesus, the righteous one, who Himself adorned His church and awaits its coming to heaven. This is described in Revelation as the marriage of the bride to her bridegroom.

Malachi 4:2 describes Jesus's righteousness this way: "But for you who revere my name, the sun of righteousness [The Messiah, Jesus Christ] will rise with healing in its rays. And you will go out and frolic like well-fed calves" (emphasis added).

The "enormous red dragon with seven heads and ten horns with seven crowns on its heads" is obviously Satan. The seven heads are believed by some scholars to be the seven hills of Rome, from which the Roman Empire's "horns," or ten provinces, ruled. These seven heads could also portray seven world powers under Satan. Some theologians believe the seven crowns are the seven kingdoms that followed the Roman regime. These symbols could also apply to Satan's powerful regime during the tribulation, which could easily encompass the radical Islamic terrorists.

The dragon's tail swept *a third of the stars out of the sky* and flung them to the earth. This is easily construed as *God's disobedient angels choosing Satan and being cast out of heaven with him*. In Isaiah and Ezekiel, one sees God's reasoning for dealing with Satan in this manner:

> *How you have fallen from heaven, morning star, son of the dawn! You have been cast down to the earth*, you who once laid low the nations! *You said* in your heart, "*I will* ascend to the heavens; *I will* raise my throne above the stars of God; *I will* sit enthroned on the mount of assembly, on the utmost heights of Mount Zaphon. *I will* ascend above the tops of the clouds; *I will* make myself like the Most High." But you are brought down to the realm of the dead, to the depths of the pit. (Isaiah 14:12–15, emphasis added)

> *You were anointed as a guardian cherub,* for so I ordained you. *You were on the holy mount of God; you walked among the fiery stones. You were blameless in your ways from the day you were created till wickedness was found in you.* Through your widespread trade you were filled with violence, and you sinned. So I drove you in disgrace from the mount of God, and I expelled you, guardian cherub, from among the fiery stones. *Your heart became proud on account of your beauty, and you corrupted your wisdom because of your splendor.* So I threw you to the earth; I made a spectacle of you before kings By your many sins and dishonest trade you have desecrated your sanctuaries. So I made a fire come out from you, and it consumed you, and I reduced you to ashes on the ground in the sight of all who were watching. All the nations who knew you are appalled at you; you have come to a horrible end and will be no more. (Ezekiel 28:14–19, emphasis added)

These are obviously descriptions of Satan, his desires, and his being cast out of heaven because he would place himself above God.

Revelation 12:5–9

Revelation 12 continues as follows:

> *She gave birth to a son, a male child, who "will rule all the nations with an iron scepter."* And her child was snatched up to God and to his throne. The woman fled into the wilderness to a place prepared for her by God, where she might be taken care of for 1,260 days. Then war broke out in heaven. Michael and his angels fought against the dragon, and the dragon and his angels fought back. But he was not strong enough, and they lost their place in heaven. The great dragon was hurled down— that ancient serpent called the devil, or Satan, who leads the whole world astray. He was hurled to the earth, and his angels with him. (Revelation 12:5–9, emphasis added)

Satan fought God, but was banned from heaven and cast down with his followers. Note also the reference to that "old serpent" called the Devil. This, of course, refers to Satan as a snake, when he was in the garden of Eden. Also recall the letter to Pergamum. Pergamum was once Satan's headquarters where he had a pagan temple, Aesculapius (the Temple of the Snake), where sacrifices were actually offered to Satan.

Jesus is described as the born "son" who "will rule all the nations with an iron scepter." The scepter of God is given to Jesus from the tribe of Judah and will never depart from Him. Jacob, in blessing his sons, said the following to Judah, whose genetic line led to Jesus: "The scepter will not depart from Judah, nor the ruler's staff from between his feet, until he to whom it belongs shall come and the obedience of the nations shall be his" (Genesis 49:10). Jesus Christ is God and rules everything in the universe.

Revelation 12:10–13

Revelation 12 continues as follows:

> Then I heard a loud voice in heaven say: "Now have come the salvation and the power and the kingdom of our God, and the authority of his Messiah. For the accuser of our brothers and sisters, who accuses them before our God day and night, has been hurled down. *They triumphed over him by the blood of the Lamb and by the word of their testimony; they did not love their lives so much as to shrink from death.* Therefore rejoice, you heavens and you who dwell in them! But woe to the earth and the sea, because the devil has gone down to you! He is filled with fury, because he knows that his time is short." *When the dragon saw that he had been hurled to the earth, he pursued the woman who had given birth to the male child.* (Revelation 12:10–13, emphasis added)

Here we see the triumph of God over Satan "by the blood of the Lamb and by the word of their testimony"—referring to the testimony of those who died for Christ and the church. However, we also see the great tribulation bringing much woe to those left on earth. Satan takes his vengeance out on the church and the Jews, who have suffered from their very beginning.

Anti-Semitism is on the rise in our day and is permitted partly because of the Jews' disobedience to God and also partly due to Satan's realization that the Jews brought the Savior into the world to conquer him. In addition, as we had mentioned, we now see in our time the "birth pains" indicating the beginning of the tribulation period. These signs include unusual world storms, hurricanes, tornadoes, droughts, floods, earthquakes, tsunamis, wars, terrorists, wanton killings, violence—and the list goes on.

Revelation 12:14–17

Revelation 12 continues as follows:

> The woman was given the two wings of a great eagle, so that she might fly to the place prepared for her in the wilderness, where she would be taken care of for a time, times and half a time, out of the serpent's reach. Then from his mouth the serpent spewed water like a river, to overtake the woman and sweep her away with the torrent. But the earth helped the woman by opening its mouth and swallowing the river that the dragon had spewed out of his mouth. *Then the dragon was enraged at the woman and went off to wage war against the rest of her offspring—those who keep God's commands and hold fast their testimony about Jesus.* (Revelation 12:14–17, emphasis added)

Zechariah 13:8–9 is relevant to these verses: "In the whole land," declares the LORD, *"two-thirds will be struck down and perish; yet one-third will be left in it.* This third I will put into the fire; I will refine them like silver and test them like gold. *They will call on my name and I will answer them; I will say, 'They are my people,' and they will say, 'The LORD is our God'"* (emphasis added). With all of the killing of humans that goes on in the world during this tribulation period, we now see that there will only be about *one-third of the Jews left*, but this is the fulfillment of God's plan as He reveals it to man.

Jews, who have been persecuted for thousands of years, will have this next epoch with Satan in power to discriminate against them for the last time. His vengeance will be very pronounced and bitter, as he will know his time is ending. Satan goes after the Jews and anyone believing in Jesus as Lord and Savior. Because God will intervene, one-third of the Jews will be able to escape Satan's grasp, but this one-third will be tested and made perfect for heaven. An interesting statistic is that 80 percent of the Jews living in Israel in our time (AD 2014) are atheists as reported by the Baptist Record paper and the Philadelphia Trumpet magazine in 2014. Perhaps that is why only one-third will go through the fire of God. However, after their trials, where will these earthbound Jews go to escape Satan? Zechariah tells us, "You will flee by my mountain valley, for it will extend to Azel. You will flee as you fled from the earthquake in the days of Uzziah king of Judah. Then the LORD my God will come, and all the holy ones with him" (Zechariah 14:5).

Some expositors believe "Azel" could pertain to Petra. This ancient city is surrounded by mountains. To get to it, one has to pass through narrow clefts, which allow only two or three people side by side to go through at a time. Petra was the capital of Edom. The following verses substantiate these Bible scholars' belief, because Jesus will rescue His own who will be hiding there: "Who is this coming from Edom, from Bozrah, with his garments stained crimson? Who is this, robed in splendor, striding forward in the greatness of his strength? 'It is I, proclaiming victory, mighty to save'" (Isaiah 63:1). Also, "He will also invade the Beautiful Land. Many countries will fall, but Edom, Moab and the leaders of Ammon will be delivered from his hand" (Daniel 11:41). So, for reasons of safety, the remaining Jews flee to "Azel," which many Bibles spell *Azal*). Edom will not fall into Satan's or his antichrist's hand.

Some expositors believe this "Azel" is the ravine mentioned in Zechariah: "You will flee by my mountain valley, for it will extend to Azel. You will flee as you fled from the earthquake in the days of

Uzziah king of Judah. Then the LORD my God will come, and all the holy ones with him" (Zechariah 14:5).

Other Bible scholars understand this to be Beth-Ezel, which became Bethany in more modem times.

Regardless of where the Israelis go, God will protect them from Satan's last attempts of persecution. These events go to the gates of Jerusalem, as Micah 1:11–12 tells us: "Pass by naked and in shame, you who live in Shaphir. Those who live in Zaanan will not come out. Beth Ezel is in mourning; it no longer protects you. Those who live in Maroth writhe in pain, waiting for relief, because disaster has come from the LORD, even to the gate of Jerusalem."

* * * * *

Revelation 13:1–4

Revelation 13 begins as follows:

> The dragon stood on the shore of the sea. And I saw a beast coming out of the sea. It had ten horns and seven heads, with ten crowns on its horns, and on each head a blasphemous name. The beast I saw resembled a leopard, but had feet like those of a bear and a mouth like that of a lion. The dragon gave the beast his power and his throne and great authority. One of the heads of the beast seemed to have had a fatal wound, but the fatal wound had been healed. *The whole world was filled with wonder and followed the beast. People worshiped the dragon because he had given authority to the beast, and they also worshiped the beast* and asked, "Who is like the beast? Who can wage war against it?" (Revelation 13:1–4, emphasis added)

This "beast coming out of the sea" is the antichrist as either a person or as one of Satan's antichrist systems. In Scripture, seas and waters usually represent people, as shown to us later in Revelation: "Then the angel said to me, 'The waters you saw, where the prostitute sits, are peoples, multitudes, nations and languages'" (Revelation 17:15).

Here we see Satan (the dragon) empowering the beast that comes out from the nations and has power over all people. The ten horns, seven heads, and ten crowns are thought to be powerful individuals, leaders of governments, and/or nations under Satan and his antichrist's rule.

One of the heads of the beast in the verses above seems to have had a fatal wound, but the fatal wound has been healed. Some theologians think that because Satan desires to imitate God, he uses similar constructs as God. He would try to fool people into believing he could raise someone from the dead.

Thus, he may falsify raising one of his leaders so that people would embrace him in wonder and awe.

Some expositors think this "beast" was one of the four world conquering powers that fell. However, now we see a new power, the Islamic religion, rising during our time here on earth. The Muslims desire to conquer the world. Several men have tried to conquer the world since the Roman Empire, but all have failed, because God had decreed that *there would only be four world-conquering nations* as described by Daniel's rendering of Nebuchadnezzar's dream:

> As for me, this mystery has been revealed to me, not because I have greater wisdom than anyone else alive, but so that Your Majesty may know the interpretation and that you may understand what went through your mind. "Your Majesty looked, and there before you stood a large statue—an enormous, dazzling statue, awesome in appearance. The head of the statue was made of pure gold, its chest and arms of silver, its belly and thighs of bronze, its legs of iron, its feet partly of iron and partly of baked clay. While you were watching, a rock was cut out, but not by human hands. It struck the statue on its feet of iron and clay and smashed them. Then the iron, the clay, the bronze, the silver and the gold were all broken to pieces and became like chaff on a threshing floor in the summer. The wind swept them away without leaving a trace. But the rock that struck

> the statue became a huge mountain and filled the whole earth. (Daniel 2:30–35)

And Daniel then provides the explanation of the dream given to him by God.

> This was the dream, and now we will interpret it to the king. Your Majesty, you are the king of kings. The God of heaven has given you dominion and power and might and glory; in your hands he has placed all mankind and the beasts of the field and the birds in the sky. Wherever they live, he has made you ruler over them all. You are that head of gold. After you, another kingdom will arise, inferior to yours. Next, a third kingdom, one of bronze, will rule over the whole earth. Finally, there will be a fourth kingdom, strong as iron—for iron breaks and smashes everything—and as iron breaks things to pieces, so it will crush and break all the others. Just as you saw that the feet and toes were partly of baked clay and partly of iron, so this will be a divided kingdom; yet it will have some of the strength of iron in it, even as you saw iron mixed with clay. As the toes were partly iron and partly clay, so this kingdom will be partly strong and partly brittle. And just as you saw the iron mixed with baked clay, so the people will be a mixture and will not remain united, any more than iron mixes with clay. In the time of those kings, the God of heaven will set up a kingdom that will never be destroyed, nor will it be left to another people. It will crush all those kingdoms and bring them to an end, but it will itself endure forever. This is the meaning of the vision of the rock cut out of a mountain, but not by human hands—a rock that broke the iron, the bronze, the clay, the silver and the gold to pieces. The great God has shown the king what will take place in the future. The dream is true and its interpretation is trustworthy. (Daniel 2:36–45)

The four conquering powers were Nebuchadnezzar, the Persians, Alexander the Great, and the Romans. The Holy Roman Empire was the last world conqueror, which, Bible scholars believe, has been *revived* somewhat in the form of the papacy. The Roman Empire adopted the Rome Universal (Catholic) Church as its national church before Rome fell in AD 476. Emblematically, the Roman Catholic Church later came under the headship of the pope. *The Roman Catholic Church assumed itself (by its own authority) to be Christ's representative on earth, but this has never been confirmed by Scripture.* Revelation's words seem to confirm this rendition of true Bible scholars' opinions, because the Roman Catholic Church exists in most countries of the world, and the pope is an international authority figure, certainly a respected figure throughout the world, whose office will be very powerful during the tribulation period under Satan.

However, the Islamic religion is the fastest growing in the world today (as of 2014), so Islam could actually be Satan's religious system that only bears some resemblance to the Roman Catholic Church. *The Baptist Record* reported that Islam is now second to Christianity in the world, including all the southern states (the Bible belt) except for South Carolina and Tennessee.

Revelation 13:5–7

The world's political, economic, and religious systems will be very powerful under Satan during the tribulation period. Satan, wanting to be like God, has anti-god personalities behind him. The antichrist will be very powerful, with a charismatic personality and charm to mislead people. God describes him here: "*The beast* was given a mouth to utter proud words and blasphemies and to exercise its authority for forty-two months. It *opened its mouth to blaspheme God, and to slander his name and his dwelling place and those who live in heaven.* It was given power to wage war against God's holy people and to conquer them. And it was given authority over every tribe, people, language and nation" (Revelation 13:5–7, emphasis added). This beast is quite probably the antichrist.

Revelation 13:8–10

Chapter 13 continues as follows: "*All inhabitants of the earth will worship the beast—all whose names have not been written in the Lamb's book of life*, the Lamb who was slain from the creation of the world. Whoever has ears, let them hear. 'If anyone is to go into captivity, into captivity they will go. If anyone is to be killed with the sword, with the sword they will be killed.' This calls for patient endurance and faithfulness on the part of God's people" (Revelation 13:8–10, emphasis added). Both Daniel and Paul foresaw the antichrist in the following verses:

> The ten horns are ten kings who will come from this kingdom. After them another king will arise, different from the earlier ones; he will subdue three kings. He will speak against the Most High and oppress his holy people and try to change the set times and the laws. The holy people will be delivered into his hands for a time, times and half a time. (Daniel 7:24–25)

> The king will do as he pleases. He will exalt and magnify himself above every god and will say unheard-of things against the God of gods. He will be successful until the time of wrath is completed, for what has been determined must take place. (Daniel 11:36)

> Don't let anyone deceive you in any way, for that day will not come until the rebellion occurs and the man of lawlessness is revealed, the man doomed to destruction. He will oppose and will exalt himself over everything that is called God or is worshiped, so that he sets himself up in God's temple, proclaiming himself to be God. (2 Thessalonians 2:3-4)

> And then the lawless one will be revealed, whom the Lord Jesus will overthrow with the breath of his mouth and destroy by the splendor of his coming. The coming of the lawless one will be in accordance with how Satan

works. He will use all sorts of displays of power through signs and wonders that serve the lie, and all the ways that wickedness deceives those who are perishing. They perish because they refused to love the truth and so be saved. (2 Thessalonians 2:8– 10)

There is much discussion among Bible students as to the nationality of the beast, the antichrist. Most biblical scholars believe the antichrist will be of Jewish origin but carefully hiding that information, because of some people's hatred for Jews. Adolph Hitler had a Jewish background, but he concealed that fact very well until it was discovered after WWII. Daniel gives us a clue in this respect by foretelling the antichrist's disregard for his ancestors: "The king will do as he pleases. He will exalt and magnify himself above every god and will say unheard-of things against the God of gods. He will be successful until the time of wrath is completed, for what has been determined must take place. He will show no regard for the gods of his ancestors or for the one desired by women, nor will he regard any god, but will exalt himself above them all" (Daniel 11:36–37). On the antichrist's ethnic background, Tim LaHaye writes, "[His] ancestry may be known only to God, but the Bible teaches that he will be a Roman-Grecian Jew, a composite man representing the peoples of the earth. This technically qualifies him to be the embodiment of all evil men."[1]

Revelation 13:11–13

Revelation 13:11–13 reads as follows:

> "Then I saw a second beast, coming out of the earth. *It* had two horns like a lamb, but it spoke like a dragon. *It* exercised all the authority of the first beast on its behalf, and made the earth and its inhabitants worship the first beast, whose fatal wound had been healed. *And it performed* great signs, even causing fire to come down from heaven to the earth in full view of the people" (emphasis added). Some expositors of Scripture believe

that this second beast, with two horns like a lamb, is a form of the papacy revived under Satan's rule. In other words, it is the church or a religious organization. Note that verse 13 says, "and it [the beast] performed great wonders or signs ..." The "it" could be a system or refer to a person. Satan's secular system has come onto the scene quietly and mildly but with much power during this time of tribulation.

Other experts claim that the "it" signifies religious power in the hands of secular authority. It quickly gains recognition and influence and then bespeaks of, and like, Satan. To repeat myself, because Islam, the Muslim religion, is booming with new adherents in the last couple of years, the religious system under Satan could very well be a combination of both.

Revelation 13:14–18

Chapter 13 continues as follows:

> Because of the signs *it* was given power to perform on behalf of the first beast, *it* deceived the inhabitants of the earth. *It* ordered them to set up an image in honor of the beast who was wounded by the sword and yet lived. The second beast was given power to give breath to the image of the first beast, so that the image could speak and cause all who refused to worship the image to be killed. *It also forced all people, great and small, rich and poor, free and slave, to receive a mark on their right hands or on their foreheads,* so that they could not buy or sell unless they had the mark, which is the name of the beast or the number of its name. This calls for wisdom. Let the person who has insight calculate the number of the beast, for it is the number of a man. That number is 666. (Revelation 13:14– 18, emphasis added)

Here we see more references to "it" presented, indicating the satanic system instituted by Satan. The meaning of the number 666 is, thus far, beyond human comprehension. The ancient Hebrew and Greek languages did not have numerical systems that separated numbers from alphabet characters. Hence, the first letter of the Hebrew alphabet was one; the second was two; and so on. For any name, it is possible to total the alphabet characters by adding their numerical value together, but because of the *various spellings* of names, *totals do not necessarily agree.* All we can say about 666 is that it is as described by verse 18: "the number of a man."

Because of the "signs," the second beast is given power to perform on behalf of the first beast, by deceiving the inhabitants of the earth. "It" orders them to *set up an image* (a statue or idol sculpture?) in honor of the beast wounded by the sword who yet lived. Satan either uses ventriloquism or has the power to make the image speak!

Satan, being the great imitator of God, *seals his constituents* in a manner similar to the way in which God did back in Revelation 7:2—"Then I saw another angel coming up from the east, having the seal of the living God. He called out in a loud voice to the four angels who had been given power to harm the land and the sea: *'Do not harm the land or the sea or the trees until we put a seal on the foreheads of the servants of our God.'* Then I heard *the number of those who were sealed: 144,000 from all the tribes of Israel"* (emphasis added).

* * * * *

4

REVELATION 14:1–17:18

> Now is the time for judgment on this world; now the prince of this world will be driven out.
>
> —John 12:31

Revelation 14:1–5

Revelation 14 takes us to the next phase of the vision:

> Then I looked, and there before me was the Lamb, standing on Mount Zion, and with him 144,000 who had his name and his Father's name written on their foreheads. And I heard a sound from heaven like the roar of rushing waters and like a loud peal of thunder. The sound I heard was like that of harpists playing their harps. And they sang a new song before the throne and before the four living creatures and the elders. No one could learn the song except the 144,000 who had been redeemed from the earth. These are those who did not defile themselves with women, for they remained virgins. They follow the Lamb wherever he goes. They were purchased from among mankind and offered as firstfruits to God and the Lamb. No lie was found in their mouths; they are blameless. (Revelation 14:1–5)

The salvation of the 144,000 (and of ours as well) was purchased by the blood of the Lamb, our Lord Jesus. The Bible preaches, "for, 'Everyone who calls on the name of the Lord will be saved'" (Romans 10:13).

Revelation 14:6–11

Revelation 14 continues as follows:

> Then I saw another angel flying in midair, and he had the eternal gospel to proclaim to those who live on the earth—to every nation, tribe, language and people. He said in a loud voice, *"Fear God and give him glory, because the hour of his judgment has come. Worship him who made the heavens, the earth, the sea and the springs of water."* A second angel followed and said, "'Fallen! Fallen is Babylon the Great,' which made all the nations drink the maddening wine of her adulteries." A third angel followed them and said in a loud voice: "If anyone worships the beast and its image and receives its mark on their forehead or on their hand, they, too, will drink the wine of God's fury, which has been poured full strength into the cup of his wrath. They will be tormented with burning sulfur in the presence of the holy angels and of the Lamb. And the smoke of their torment will rise for ever and ever. There will be no rest day or night for those who worship the beast and its image, or for anyone who receives the mark of its name." (Revelation 14:6–11, emphasis added))

This announcement of evangelism (this angel had the *eternal gospel to proclaim*) comes just before Babylon the great falls, so one may assume the gospel will be preached during the "great" tribulation period.

"Babylon" is believed to be a symbolic reference to the world's decadent, immoral, political, and religious world systems under the antichrist. We see this illustrated for us again in Revelation 17 and 18.

The name written on her forehead was a mystery: BABYLON THE GREAT THE MOTHER OF PROSTITUTES AND OF THE ABOMINATIONS OF THE EARTH. (Revelation 17:5)

With a mighty voice he shouted: *"'Fallen! Fallen is Babylon the Great!'* She has become a dwelling for demons and a haunt for every impure spirit, a haunt for every unclean bird, a haunt for every unclean and detestable animal. *For all the nations have drunk the maddening wine of her adulteries. The kings of the earth committed adultery with her, and the merchants of the earth grew rich from her excessive luxuries."* (Revelation 18:2–3, emphasis added)

Revelation 14:12–16

The next verses in chapter 14 are as follows:

> This calls for patient endurance on the part of the people of God who keep his commands and remain faithful to Jesus. Then I heard a voice from heaven say, *"Write this: Blessed are the dead who die in the Lord from now on."* "Yes," says the Spirit, "they will rest from their labor, for their deeds will follow them." *I looked, and there before me was a white cloud, and seated on the cloud was one like a son of man with a crown of gold on his head and a sharp sickle in his hand.* Then another angel came out of the temple and called in a loud voice to him who was sitting on the cloud, "Take your sickle and reap, because the time to reap has come, for the harvest of the earth is ripe." So he who was seated on the cloud swung his sickle over the earth, and the earth was harvested. (Revelation 14:12–16, emphasis added)

Verse 13 gives us the second beatitude (blessing) of Revelation: "Blessed are the dead who die in the Lord from now on." As this vision of the tribulation continues, we see rest for those individuals who die in the name of Jesus. However, the one "seated on the cloud was one like a son of man with a crown of gold on his head and a sharp sickle in his hand" *can be none other than Jesus Christ Himself*: "The Son of

Man will send out his angels, and they will weed out of his kingdom everything that causes sin and all who do evil" (Matthew 13:41).

Revelation 14:17–20

It is here, starting at Revelation 14:17, where most Bible scholars believe Armageddon begins.

> *Another angel came out of the temple in heaven, and he too had a sharp sickle.* Still another angel, who had charge of the fire, came from the altar and called in a loud voice to him who had the sharp sickle, "Take your sharp sickle and gather the clusters of grapes from the earth's vine, because its grapes are ripe." *The angel swung his sickle on the earth, gathered its grapes and threw them into the great winepress of God's wrath.* They were trampled in the winepress outside the city, *and blood flowed out of the press, rising as high as the horses' bridles for a distance of 1,600 stadia.* (Revelation 14:17–20, emphasis added)

The trampling of grapes in the Old Testament generally symbolically signifies God's wrath being carried out. Sixteen hundred stadia translates to approximately 180 miles.

Joel's prophetic description seems to fit this situation exactly: "Come quickly, all you nations from every side, and assemble there. Bring down your warriors, LORD! 'Let the nations be roused; let them advance into the Valley of Jehoshaphat, for there I will sit to judge all the nations on every side. Swing the sickle, for the harvest is ripe. Come, trample the grapes, for the winepress is full and the vats overflow—so great is their wickedness!' Multitudes, multitudes in the valley of decision! For the day of the LORD is near in the valley of decision" (Joel 3:11–14). God calls the nations to come together for their just recompense in the "valley of decision." Jehoshaphat translates as "Jehovah's judgment."

Joel's "valley of decision" is believed to be Har Megiddo (Armageddon). This deep ravine or valley extends from just outside of Jerusalem to the Mount of Olives, where Satan and his human armies will be defeated. This designation by Joel, "the valley of decision" or "the Valley of Jehoshaphat," appears to be a fitting description, because Zechariah 14:4 also tells us about Christ's touching down on earth: "On that day his feet will stand on the Mount of Olives, east of Jerusalem, and the Mount of Olives will be split in two from east to west, forming a great valley, with half of the mountain moving north and half moving south." The Mount of Olives splits, forming a great valley where the blood will flow *as high as the horses' bridles.*

The above prophecy, where Jesus is predicted to come and defeat the human armies and demons of Satan, matches perfectly Joel's revelation and Zechariah's valley of decision.

We see God's wrath extended outside of His holy city because blood flowing inside of His holy city would defile it. We are told in Hebrews: "The high priest carries the blood of animals into the Most Holy Place as a sin offering, but the bodies are burned outside the camp" (Hebrews 13:11). The high priest carries the blood of animals into the "Most Holy Place" as a sin offering, but the bodies are burned outside the camp. And so *Jesus also suffered outside the city gate* to make the people holy through his own blood.

The author of the book of Hebrews is unknown, but the experts believe it to be either Barnabas or possibly Apollo. Both of these men were very familiar with Christ's teaching, and both traveled with Paul.

The Lord Jesus was crucified outside the city of Jerusalem on a hillock named the Skull. This particular hillock does resemble a skull in some very old pictures. According to John 19:17, "Carrying his own cross, he went out to the place of the Skull (which in Aramaic is called Golgotha)."

Zechariah gives some prophetic information about Jerusalem's terrible attack.

> A day of the LORD is coming, Jerusalem, when your possessions will be plundered and divided up within your very walls. I will gather all the nations to Jerusalem to fight against it; the city will be captured, the houses ransacked, and the women raped. Half of the city will go into exile, but the rest of the people will not be taken from the city. Then the LORD will go out and fight against those

nations, as he fights on a day of battle. On that day his feet will stand on the Mount of Olives, east of Jerusalem, and the Mount of Olives will be split in two from east to west, forming a great valley, with half of the mountain moving north and half moving south. (Zechariah 14:1–4)

In addition to the above, Joel finishes this discourse concerning Jerusalem:

> *"The sun and moon will be darkened, and the stars no longer shine. The LORD will roar from Zion and thunder from Jerusalem; the earth and the heavens will tremble.* But the LORD will be a refuge for his people, a stronghold for the people of Israel. 'Then you will know that I, the LORD your God, dwell in Zion, my holy hill. Jerusalem will be holy; never again will foreigners invade her'" (Joel 3:15–17, emphasis added).

* * * * *

Revelation 15:1–4

Revelation 15 begins with another sign.

> I saw in heaven another great and marvelous sign: seven angels with the seven last plagues—last, because with them God's wrath is completed. And I saw what looked like a sea of glass glowing with fire and, standing beside the sea, those who had been victorious over the beast and its image and over the number of its name. They held harps given them by God and sang the song of God's servant Moses and of the Lamb: *"Great and marvelous are your deeds, Lord God Almighty. Just and true are your ways, King of the nations. Who will not fear you, Lord, and bring glory to your name? For you alone are holy.* All nations will come and worship before you, for your righteous acts have been revealed." (Revelation 15:1–4, emphasis added)

After the trampling of the wine press in chapter 14, we now see *seven angels given the last seven plagues to finish God's wrath upon disobedient, unbelieving humanity as well as upon the antichrist and Satan.* However, with the finishing of God's wrath, the victorious in Christ sing a song of love to God Almighty for His marvelous work. The "Song of Moses" begins with these first seven verses, found at Exodus:

> Then Moses and the Israelis sang this song to the LORD: "I will sing to the LORD, for he is highly exalted. Both horse and driver he has hurled into the sea. "The LORD is my strength and my defense; he has become my salvation. He is my God, and I will praise him, my father's God, and I will exalt him. The LORD is a warrior; the LORD is his name. Pharaoh's chariots and his army he has hurled into the sea. The best of Pharaoh's officers are drowned in the Red Sea. The deep waters have covered them; they sank to the depths like a stone. Your right hand, LORD, was majestic in power. Your right hand, LORD, shattered the enemy. "In the greatness of your majesty you threw down those who opposed you. You unleashed your burning anger; it consumed them like stubble." (Exodus 15:1– 7)

It is a fitting hymn to sing in praise to God.

Revelation 15:5–8

Revelation 15 continues as follows:

> And after that I looked, and, behold, the temple of the tabernacle of the testimony in heaven was opened: And the seven angels came out of the temple, having the seven plagues, clothed in pure and white linen, and having their breasts girded with golden girdles. *And one of the four living creatures gave to the seven angels seven golden bowls full of the wrath of God who lives forever and ever,* And the temple was filled with smoke from the glory of

God, and from his power; and no man was able to enter into the temple, till the seven plagues of the seven angels were fulfilled. (Revelation 15:5–8, emphasis added)

The-seven angels with the last seven plaques come out of the heavenly temple and they are given *seven golden bowls, filled with the wrath of God. The heavenly temple is filled with the glory of God* as the seven angels go to do their appointed work.

* * * * *

Revelation 16:1–2

The wrath of God continues as the first angel pours his bowl on the earth:

"Then I heard a loud voice from the temple saying to the seven angels, "Go, pour out the seven bowls of God's wrath on the earth." *The first angel went and poured out his bowl on the land, and ugly, festering sores broke out on the people who had the mark of the beast and worshiped its image*" (Revelation 16:1–2, emphasis added).

The first bowl of God's fury brings festering, ugly sores on people, which reminds us of the boils and abscesses of the Egyptian plague: "Then the LORD said to Moses and Aaron, 'Take handfuls of soot from a furnace and have Moses toss it into the air in the presence of Pharaoh. It will become fine dust over the whole land of Egypt, and festering boils will break out on people and animals throughout the land.' So they took soot from a furnace and stood before Pharaoh. Moses tossed it into the air, and festering boils broke out on people and animals. The magicians could not stand before Moses because of the boils that were on them and on all the Egyptians" (Exodus 9:8–11). Moreover, we have seen the effect of these painful sores, when Satan was allowed to persecute Job: "So Satan went out from the presence of the LORD and afflicted Job with painful sores from the soles of his feet to the crown of his head" (Job 2:7).

Here are a few excerpts from Job's experience: "Night pierces my bones; my gnawing pains never rest" (Job 30:17); "I go about blackened, but not by the sun; I stand up in the assembly and cry for help" (Job 30:28); and "My skin grows black and peels; my body burns with fever" (Job 30:30). These sores and boils are thought to be the Arabs' black leprosy, termed *elephantiasis* by the Greeks. Its renders the skin scabrous, dark, and furrowed all over with tubercles like that of an elephant's skin. This loathsome and most afflicting disease comes with intolerable itching and pain. This disease is certainly not very pleasant to get!

Revelation 16:3–7

The second angel pours his bowl on the sea with the third angel pouring his bowl on the rivers and springs of water.

> The second angel poured out his bowl on the sea, and it turned into blood like that of a dead person, and every living thing in the sea died. The third angel poured out his bowl on the rivers and springs of water, and they became blood. Then I heard the angel in charge of the waters say: "You are just in these judgments, O Holy One, you who are and who were; for they have shed the blood of your holy people and your prophets, and you have given them blood to drink as they deserve." And I heard the altar respond: "Yes, Lord God Almighty, true and just are your judgments." (Revelation 16:3–7)

The second angel's bowl turns the sea into blood, and everything in the sea dies. This would certainly *not* help the food situation for the remaining people.

Again, this prophecy reminds us of Egypt: "The fish in the Nile died, and the river smelled so bad that the Egyptians could not drink its water. Blood was everywhere in Egypt" (Exodus 7:21). The Egyptians held the Nile sacred and annually sacrificed children to their gods of the river. God might have designed this blood plague as a punishment for such idolatry and cruelty, as well as to show the baseness of those elements which they revered. In all ways, the punishments brought upon them bore a strict analogy to their crimes against God. God's wrath is justified, in all that He does. Humankind's foolishness is refusing to acknowledge God's substantive warranting rights. Most of the time, humankind does not even consider God.

Revelation 16:8–11

Revelation 16 continues as follows:

> The fourth angel poured out his bowl on the sun, and the sun was allowed to scorch people with fire. *They were seared by the intense heat and they cursed the name of God, who had control over these plagues, but they refused to repent and glorify him.* The fifth angel poured out his bowl on the throne of the beast, and its kingdom was plunged into darkness. People gnawed their tongues in agony and cursed the God of heaven because of their pains and their sores, but they refused to repent of what they had done. (Revelation 16:8–11, emphasis added)

People gnawed their tongues in agony and cursed the God of heaven because of their pains and their sores, but *they refused to repent or seek forgiveness* from the only God.

Again, people have become so heinous that they refuse to change or ask for God's mercy. They continue to blaspheme God, in defiance of their plight. Perhaps that is their way of justifying blaming God for *their* evil ways.

Revelation 16:12–15

Revelation 16:8–11 says,

> The sixth angel poured out his bowl on the great river Euphrates, and its water was dried up to prepare the way for the kings from the East. Then I saw three impure

> spirits that looked like frogs; they came out of the mouth of the dragon, out of the mouth of the beast and out of the mouth of the false prophet. They are demonic spirits that perform signs, and they go out to the kings of the whole world, to gather them for the battle on the great day of God Almighty. "Look, I come like a thief! Blessed is the one who stays awake and remains clothed, so as not to go naked and be shamefully exposed."

If one looks at a map, the Euphrates River is a barrier to armies coming from the east. I have read somewhere that this river has an average depth of ten to twelve feet at its deepest. So, the drying up of the Euphrates would allow most of the Arab countries to very quickly attack Israel.

Three demonic spirits appear. They are able to perform signs and wonders to convince people to fight the Israelis (and God). Jesus again warns that He comes to earth unexpectedly, just before the battle of Armageddon. *Christ had already come for the born-again ones, but He did not touch the earth. We will meet Him in the clouds.* As 1 Thessalonians 4:15–17 tells us,

> According to the Lord's word, we tell you that we who are still alive, who are left until the coming of the Lord, will certainly not precede those who have fallen asleep. For the Lord himself will come down from heaven, with a loud command, with the voice of the archangel and with the trumpet call of God, and the dead in Christ will rise first. After that, we who are still alive and are left will be caught up together with them in the clouds to meet the Lord in the air. And so we will be with the Lord forever

Revelation 16:16–21

Revelation 16 continues as follows:

> Then they gathered the kings together to the place that in Hebrew is called Armageddon. The seventh angel

poured out his bowl into the air, and out of the temple came a loud voice from the throne, saying, "It is done!" Then there came flashes of lightning, rumblings, peals of thunder and a severe earthquake. No earthquake like it has ever occurred since mankind has been on earth, so tremendous was the quake. The great city split into three parts, and the cities of the nations collapsed. *God remembered Babylon the Great and gave her the cup filled with the wine of the fury of his wrath.* Every island fled away and the mountains could not be found. *From the sky huge hailstones, each weighing about a hundred pounds, fell on people. And they cursed God on account of the plague of hail, because the plague was so terrible.* (Revelation 16:16–21, emphasis added)

According to this prophecy, the kings and their armies will gather at Armageddon, the valley of Har Megiddo. It is here that the bloodiest battle of the earth will take place. However, God Himself will fight for His cause so that all will know He alone is God!

This last earthquake will completely devastate the earth, and one-hundred- pound hailstones will follow it. Zechariah says, "A prophecy: The word of the LORD concerning Israel. The LORD, who stretches out the heavens, who lays the foundation of the earth, and who forms the human spirit within a person, declares: "I am going to make Jerusalem a cup that sends all the surrounding peoples reeling. Judah will be besieged as well as Jerusalem. On that day, when all the nations of the earth are gathered against her, I will make Jerusalem an immovable rock for all the nations. All who try to move it will injure themselves" (Zechariah 12:1–3).

* * * * *

Next, in Revelation 17, we will see the great prostitute, or harlot, representing the world church, which will lead many people down the wrong path. To understand why Babylon and Rome are the symbolic center of this statement and God's wrath, we have to go back in history.

After Adam and Eve's rejection from the garden of Eden, Satan must have been busy, because in a very short time humankind had become so evil that God wanted to wipe His creation off the face of the earth. According to the genealogies listed in Genesis 5, only 1,676 years had passed from Adam to the flood, and Genesis 6:5–7 tells us, "The LORD saw how great the wickedness of the human race had become on the earth, and that every inclination of the thoughts of the human heart was only evil all the time. The LORD regretted that he had made human beings on the earth, and his heart was deeply troubled. So the LORD said, 'I will wipe from the face of the earth the human race I have created—and with them the animals, the birds and the creatures that move along the ground—for I regret that I have made them.'"

Fortunately for us, Genesis 6:8 informs that "Noah found favor in the eyes of the LORD." Because of Noah's righteousness, God had mercy on humankind. The historical record reveals that after the flood, according to Genesis, Noah planted a vineyard. To celebrate the crop having come in, chapters 9 and 10 tell us that Noah makes some wine, but things do not always go right, and God's will will be done.

> Noah, a man of the soil, proceeded to plant a vineyard. When he drank some of its wine, he became drunk and lay uncovered inside his tent. Ham, the father of Canaan, saw his father naked and told his two brothers outside. *But Shem and Japheth took a garment and laid it across their shoulders; then they walked in backward and covered their father's naked body. Their faces were turned the other way so that they would not see their father naked.* When Noah awoke from his wine and found out what his youngest son had done to him, he said, "Cursed be Canaan! The lowest of slaves will he be to his brothers." (Genesis 9:20–25, emphasis added)

Note that *Ham apparently ridiculed his drunken, naked father*, but both Shem and Japheth did not look at their naked father. Because of Ham's indiscretion, many of his grandchildren and great grandchildren (even descendants today) are forever disobedient to God.

As Paul Harvey would say, "the rest of the story" comes to us in Genesis 10:6–12, which follows:

> The sons of Ham: Cush, Egypt, Put and Canaan. The sons of Cush: Seba, Havilah, Sabtah, Raamah and Sabteka. The sons of Raamah: Sheba and Dedan. Cush was the father of Nimrod, who became a mighty warrior on the earth. He was a mighty hunter *before* the LORD; that is why it is said, "Like Nimrod, a mighty hunter before the LORD." The first centers of his kingdom were Babylon, Uruk, Akkad and Kalneh, in Shinar. From that land he went to Assyria, where he built Nineveh, Rehoboth Ir, Calah and Resen, which is between Nineveh and Calah—which is the great city. (Emphasis added)

First, understand that ancient Hebrew is difficult to translate, and modem language experts now say that the word *before* in verse 9 should have been translated as "*against* the Lord." This is more easily understood with the knowledge that the name *Nimrod* literally translates as "rebel" or "lawless one." Genesis 9:1 tells us, "Then God blessed Noah and his sons, saying to them, "Be fruitful and increase in number and fill the earth.""

However, we just read Nimrod, and his followers did not want to disperse across the world or obey God. Nimrod's empire stretched as far as Erech, Accad, and Calah on the Persian Gulf. According to Genesis, "They said to each other, '*Come, let's make bricks and bake them thoroughly.*' They used brick instead of stone, and tar for mortar. *Then they said, 'Come, let us build ourselves a city, with a tower that reaches to the heavens, so that we may make a name for ourselves*; otherwise we will be scattered over the face of the whole earth'" (Genesis 11:3–4, emphasis added). These people were aware of Noah, the flood, and God. Being disobedient, they deliberately decided to build with both mud and kiln-dried bricks, using tar as mortar, in case God would send another flood. However, God decided to confuse the language to force them to disperse from that place and populate the world. Genesis 11:7–9 says, "'Come, let us go down and confuse their language so they will not understand each other.'

So the LORD scattered them from there over all the earth, and they stopped building the city. *That is why it was called Babel—because there the LORD confused the language of the whole world.* From there the LORD scattered them over the face of the whole earth." (emphasis added)

The world at that time still spoke only one language, and people settled in the Mesopotamia-Mediterranean area, only a few hundred miles from where the ark landed on Mount Ararat. Even in those early days, people did not want any part of God. These people under Satan's influence built a city named Bab El (meaning "gateway to God"). Reading between the lines, apparently the people of Bab El started a tower to try to reach into heaven so that they could *deal with God directly*. Satan's headquarters started at Bab El, and he led his followers to build what *eventually* became the Tower of Babylon. Under Satan, these people disobeyed God by not wanting to scatter over the earth. The name Bab El became Babel after God saw the people's unwillingness to follow His command to disperse and populate the earth. God decided to confound the singularity of language in order to force the scattering.

The name Babel, after some years, changed again to Babylon.

Here is some historical information to help explain the paganism that started in the early Christian church as well as how it evolved.

Nimrod (the mighty hunter "against" the Lord), rather than obeying God and moving on, founded the first dynasty and built the first cities. In the course of conquering the area and building his empire, Nimrod married a woman named Semiramis. She became the Queen of Babylon and had a son, whom she named Tammuz. Semiramis wanted more power, and knowing people worshipped gods, she claimed to be the queen of heaven, because she was the mother of Tammuz, whom she claimed was a god. People then worshiped her and Tammuz, but Nimrod saw her power play and threatened to expose her. Semiramis devised a very complex scheme and had Nimrod killed. She than instigated a religion in which her son was worshipped as a god, as was she, as his mother. Some traditions say she lusted after and married her own son. We do not know all the details, but apparently Tammuz sought more power, and Semiramis decided to have him killed. Tammuz discovered her plan, had her killed, and became the sole god to his followers. This was the beginning of what we now know as Babylon.

In Egypt, the mother-child cult was Isia and Horus. Greece named them Aphrodite and Eros. In Rome, this pair was worshiped as Venus and Cupid. One of China's cults named them Mother Shing Moo and her child.

To give you an idea of how much Satan had accomplished *in misleading people*, they actually believed Semiramis *to be* the mother of God, and that Tammuz was God. There is some evidence given in ancient writings that the "sign of the cross" given by Catholics was originally the sign of a "T" for Tammuz. People had placed idols of Tammuz everywhere, including at crossroads. This sign was made when people prayed to these roadside idols of/to Tammuz.

God took Ezekiel aside to show him how evil some of the Israel priests had become and how big this belief in Tammuz really was. According to Ezekiel,

> And there before me was the glory of the God of Israel, as in the vision I had seen in the plain. Then he said to me, "Son of man, look toward the north." So I looked, and in the entrance north of the gate of the altar I saw this idol of jealousy. And he said to me, "Son of man, do you see what they are doing—the utterly detestable things the Israelites are doing here, things that will drive me far from my sanctuary? But you will see things that are even more detestable." Then he brought me to the entrance to the court. I looked, and I saw a hole in the wall. He said to me, *"Son of man, now dig into the wall." So I dug into the wall and saw a doorway there. And he said to me, "Go in and see the wicked and detestable things they are doing here." So I went in and looked, and I saw portrayed all over the walls all kinds of crawling things and unclean animals and all the idols of Israel.* In front of them stood seventy elders of Israel, and Jaazaniah son of Shaphan was standing among them. Each had a censer in his hand, and a fragrant cloud of incense was rising. He said to me, "Son of man, have you seen what the elders of Israel are doing in the darkness, each at the

shrine of his own idol? *They say, 'The LORD does not see us; the LORD has forsaken the land.'"* Again, he said, "You will see them doing things that are even more detestable." *Then he brought me to the entrance of the north gate of the house of the LORD, and I saw women sitting there, mourning the god Tammuz.* He said to me, "Do you see this, son of man? You will see things that are even more detestable than this." *He then brought me into the inner court of the house of the LORD, and there at the entrance to the temple, between the portico and the altar, were about twenty-five men. With their backs toward the temple of the LORD and their faces toward the east, they were bowing down to the sun in the east.* He said to me, "Have you seen this, son of man? Is it a trivial matter for the people of Judah to do the detestable things they are doing here? Must they also fill the land with violence and continually arouse my anger? Look at them putting the branch to their nose! Therefore I will deal with them in anger; *I will not look on them with pity or spare them. Although they shout in my ears, I will not listen to them."* (Ezekiel 8:4–18, emphasis added)

Jeremiah 7:17–19 also relates the adopted evil ways of Semiramis and Tammuz, worshipped by many Israelite people: *"Do you not see what they are doing in the towns of Judah and in the streets of Jerusalem? The children gather wood, the fathers light the fire, and the women knead the dough and make cakes to offer to the Queen of Heaven.* They pour out drink offerings to other gods to arouse my anger. But am I the one they are provoking? declares the LORD. Are they not rather harming themselves, to their own shame?" (emphasis added).

Jeremiah 7:30–34 further informs us,

The people of Judah have done evil in my eyes, declares the LORD. They have set up their detestable idols in the house that bears my Name and have defiled it. *They have built*

> *the high places of Topheth in the Valley of Ben Hinnom to burn their sons and daughters in the fire—something I did not command, nor did it enter my mind.* So beware, the days are coming, declares the LORD, when people will no longer call it Topheth or the Valley of Ben Hinnom, but the Valley of Slaughter, for they will bury the dead in Topheth until there is no more room. Then the carcasses of this people will become food for the birds and the wild animals, and there will be no one to frighten them away. I will bring an end to the sounds of joy and gladness and to the voices of bride and bridegroom in the towns of Judah and the streets of Jerusalem, for the land will become desolate. (Jeremiah 7:30–34, emphasis added)

These evil practices were everywhere and influenced people greatly. *Even the Jews* living in Egypt, in Migdol, Tahpanhes, and Memphis, *were taken in by the worship of evil idols*. Jeremiah tried to warn these people of God's anger, and even today, we see the result of the satanic influence they derived through their false belief, as described by Jeremiah.

> Then all the men who knew that their wives were burning incense to other gods, along with all the women who were present—a large assembly—and all the people living in Lower and Upper Egypt, said to Jeremiah, *"We will not listen to the message you have spoken to us in the name of the LORD! We will certainly do everything we said we would: We will burn incense to the Queen of Heaven and will pour out drink offerings to her just as we and our ancestors, our kings and our officials did in the towns of Judah and in the streets of Jerusalem.* At that time we had plenty of food and were well off and suffered no harm. But ever since we stopped burning incense to the Queen of Heaven and pouring out drink offerings to her, we have had nothing and have been perishing by sword and famine." *The women added, "When we burned incense to the Queen of Heaven and poured out drink offerings to*

her, did not our husbands know that we were making cakes impressed with her image and pouring out drink offerings to her?" (Jeremiah 44:15–19, emphasis added)

As was mentioned above, Ham's descendants continued to be disobedient adversaries of the Israelis. Genesis 10:13–20 tells us the family lines of Ham's sons: "Egypt was the father of the Ludites, Anamites, Lehabites, Naphtuhites, Pathrusites, Kasluhites (from whom the Philistines came) and Caphtorites. Canaan was the father of Sidon his firstborn, and of the Hittites, Jebusites, Amorites, Girgashites, Hivites, Arkites, Sinites, Arvadites, Zemarites and Hamathites. Later the Canaanite clans scattered and the borders of Canaan reached from Sidon toward Gerar as far as Gaza, and then toward Sodom, Gomorrah, Admah and Zeboyim, as far as Lasha. These are the sons of Ham by their clans and languages, in their territories and nations." One interesting thought here is that the Arabs of today descend from the clans, the listed names, mentioned above. These progeny of Ham still live in the same regions and appear to be very radical and demonic in their hatred of Jews and Christians. They could *possibly* be a part of the curse placed on Ham.

There appears to be no help for those who rely on themselves and who are not willing to listen and learn truth. The city of Babylon was the seat of Satan worship until it fell in 539 BC to the Persians. From Babylon, Satan worship spread to Phoenicia under the name of Ashteroth and Tammuz. From Phoenicia, it traveled to Pergamum in Asia Minor. John's admonition to the church at Pergamum informs us, "I know where you live—where Satan has his throne. Yet you remain true to my name. You did not renounce your faith in me, not even in the days of Antipas, my faithful witness, who was put to death in your city—where Satan lives" (Revelation 2:13).

* * * * *

Revelation 17 to 19 shows us the destruction of Babylon. This ancient city, Babylon of Mesopotamia, was a political, commercial, and religious center for a world empire under Nimrod. Beginning with Bab El becoming Babel and later Babylon, Babylon was noted for its luxury and moral decadence. The word *Babylon* appears in the Bible 284 times, but the words *Babylon the Great* appear in only seven verses. According to some scholars, Babylon is used in Revelation to represent the center of opposition to God and His people. According to others, it represents the complete political and religious system of the world in general, under the rule of the antichrist.

Revelation 17:1–6

Revelation 17 starts as follows:

> One of the seven angels who had the seven bowls came and said to me, "Come, I will show you the punishment of the great prostitute, who sits by many waters. *With her the kings of the earth committed adultery, and the inhabitants of the earth were intoxicated with the wine of her adulteries.*" Then the angel carried me away in the Spirit into a wilderness. There I saw a woman sitting on a scarlet beast that was covered with blasphemous names and had seven heads and ten horns. The woman was dressed in purple and scarlet, and was glittering with gold, precious stones and pearls. She held a golden cup in her hand, filled with abominable things and the filth of her adulteries. The name written on her forehead was a mystery: BABYLON THE GREAT THE MOTHER OF PROSTITUTES AND OF THE ABOMINATIONS OF THE EARTH. *I saw that the woman was drunk with the blood of God's holy people, the blood of those who bore testimony to Jesus.* When I saw her, I was greatly astonished. (Revelation 17:1–6, emphasis added)

Fornication is defined as sex between an unmarried man and woman. The original Greek word implies adultery. Adultery is a sin-act. Most experts agree that this may refer to not only the world perpetrating sin in/by *the false church*, but also *Israel having committed sins by abandoning God for idols and false worship.* Symbolically in the Bible, Israel is the wife of God. Jesus Christ's church is His bride to be. *Thus, we see the figurative connection between the prostitute and the church.* The "great prostitute," under satanic rule, covered the whole world. This false church ("who sits by many waters") conveyed evil to many peoples and nations. *Waters*, in this case, means "peoples": "Then the angel said to me, 'The waters you saw, where the prostitute sits, are peoples, multitudes, nations and languages'" (Revelation 17:15).

The scarlet beast's seven heads and ten horns may refer to nations or kings at the end time. These people under Satan's rule follow the antichrist's lead to destruction.

"The name written on her forehead was a mystery" could possibly refer to harlots of ancient times who wrote their names on their foreheads and on their houses. I assume this was done to get more trade by advertising. Thee mystery is thought to be *not* connected to the prostitutes, but to "Babylon the Great." "BABYLON THE GREAT, THE MOTHER OF PROSTITUTES AND OF THE ABOMINATIONS OF THE EARTH" is alleged, by scholars, to be the earthly religious system under satanic rule. As was shown earlier, Babylon, built by the rebel, Nimrod, and his wife, Semiramis, was the beginning of much false religion and abomination that filled the earth. Its corruption and evil sidetracked individuals from the truth of God. However, much of this abomination was introduced and carried on by Constantine's Church of Rome and brought down to us. Much of that evil exists in many of our modern Reformed churches. We say this because the Roman Catholic Church decreed that Sunday was to be Christians' Sabbath, Easter would be resurrection day, and Christmas would celebrate Christ's birthday. Nowhere in Scripture does it say that we are to celebrate these days. Christmas and Easter gave Satan a chance to introduce evil, via the Easter bunny and Santa Claus and presents, to distract people from the truth. The Reformed church remembrance is the supper celebration with the Communion bread and wine

Revelation 17:7–8

The next verses of Revelation 17 read as follows: "Then the angel said to me: "Why are you astonished? I will explain to you the mystery of the woman and of the beast she rides, which has the seven heads and ten horns. The beast, which you saw, once was, now is not, and yet will come up out of the Abyss and go to its destruction. *The inhabitants of the earth whose names have not been written in the book of life from the creation of the world will be astonished when they see the beast, because it once was, now is not, and yet will come*" (Revelation 17:7–8, emphasis added). The woman drunk with the blood of God's holy people and those who bore testimony of Jesus is, of course, "BABYLON THE GREAT, THE MOTHER OF PROSTITUTES AND OF THE ABOMINATIONS OF THE EARTH." Most expositors of Scripture believe this statement refers to the system of world religions started by Satan in Babylon.

Again, I interject that Islam has killed untold numbers of people (and continues to do so), so Islam could possibly be used by Satan during the end of the tribulation. Radical Muslims are a very violent and murderous people in today's world who are possibly even demonized by Satan.

Most commentaries believe the "beast" to be kingdoms or nations, those who have endorsed the false religions for prophet or gain. This beast, which "once was, now is not, and yet will come" reflects Satan's corrupted, ecclesiastical world church, started at Babylon under Nimrod and Semiramis. Most biblical scholars include Babylon with Rome, under Emperor Constantine, because Rome *once was, now is not, and yet will come* (to power again) under Satan's rule in the great tribulation. Perhaps it will come with Islamic belief and Sharia law.

Revelation 17:9–14

Revelation 17 continues:

> *This calls for a mind with wisdom.* The seven heads are seven hills on which the woman sits. They are also seven kings. Five have fallen, one is, the other has not yet come; but when he does come, he must remain for only a little while. The beast who once was, and now is not, is an eighth king. He belongs to the seven and is going to his destruction. The ten horns you saw are ten kings who have not yet received a kingdom, but who for one hour will

receive authority as kings along with the beast. They have one purpose and will give their power and authority to the beast. *They will wage war against the Lamb, but the Lamb will triumph over them because he is Lord of lords and King of kings—and with him will be his called, chosen and faithful followers.* (Revelation 17:9–14, emphasis added)

Some expositors of Scripture see the seven heads as seven mountains (hills), referring to Rome, which was built on seven hills. There is a discrepancy, though, regarding the seven kings, five of which have fallen and one of which is yet to come. From the description given here, these five fallen could easily be the five ancient empires of Egypt, Assyria, Babylonia, Persia, and Greece. What fits here is that the Roman, Babylonian, or Muslim empires have yet to come. The heritage left by these kingdoms' people will wage war with the Lamb (Jesus), but the Lamb will triumph. *Jesus is the King of Kings and Lord of Lords.*

Revelation 17:15–18

Revelation 17:15–18 concludes the chapter: "Then the angel said to me, 'The waters you saw, where the prostitute sits, are peoples, multitudes, nations and languages. The beast and the ten horns you saw will hate the prostitute. They will bring her to ruin and leave her naked; they will eat her flesh and burn her with fire. *For God has put it into their hearts to accomplish his purpose* by agreeing to hand over to the beast their royal authority, until God's words are fulfilled. The woman you saw is the great city that rules over the kings of the earth'" (emphasis added). The beast will bring the ecclesiastical system under Satan's control to persecute the "waters," which represent people from all over the world. The woman, as the great city, is where Satan has his headquarters. It is from here that the world's carnage against God comes, until God puts His enemies, Satan and the antichrist, down for all time.

* * * * *

5

Revelation 18:1–22:21

> Therefore do not be foolish, but understand what the Lord's will is.
>
> —Ephesians 5:17

Chapter 18 of Revelation gives us the downfall of the world's political and economic systems. Again the city of Babylon is mentioned, but it seems to encompass the meaning of being many cities or world systems. Saddam Hussein was rebuilding Babylon to its former glory, so there is a possibility the *old* Babylon is included in the world's evil cities. Perhaps the mention of Babylon is a reference to show its evil past, because old Babylon was originally Babel and, before that, Bab El, where God dispersed the evil people to populate the world. Because of God having *dispersed* the people, it does *not* appear to be the *center* of world power activity and leaders. Nevertheless, because this *was* the very first center and the beginning of humanism and the defiance of God, as well as, at one time, Satan's headquarters, it could very well be the center of Satan's rule.

Revelation 18:1–3

Revelation 18:1–3 says, "After this I saw another angel coming down from heaven. He had great authority, and the earth was illuminated by his splendor. With a mighty voice he shouted: '"Fallen! Fallen is Babylon the Great!" She has become a dwelling for demons and a haunt for every impure spirit, a haunt for every unclean bird, a haunt for every unclean and detestable animal. For all the nations have drunk the maddening wine of her adulteries. The kings of the earth committed adultery with her, and the merchants of the earth grew rich from her excessive luxuries.'" Many Bible scholars believe Babylon is a symbol of the world's religious systems. However, "all the nations have drunk the maddening wine of her adulteries" could easily pertain to the Roman Catholic Church. The Christian religion (according to statistics from 2013) is still the largest religion in the world at 33.4 percent of the population. Roman Catholics are 16.9 percent, but Catholicism has dwindled greatly from its past glory. Islam now consists of 22.7 percent of the world's population, and it is growing fast. The papacy's influence on world empires and peoples, reflect the Roman Catholic portrayal of the Bible, which in many cases does not agree with Scripture. I am not anti-Catholic in any way, and there are many good Christian Catholics. I present these facts only because many biblical scholars agree concerning this situation.

Herbert Armstrong wrote an article for *Plain Truth Magazine* in 1951 entitled "The Pope plans to move the Vatican." This article describes how powerful the Roman Catholic Church is by referring to its worldly political power. He states that the "real objective of the Catholic political power is precisely the same as the goals of communism and fascism—to gain dominance, control and rule the whole world." He relates that the papacy is a *state*, and he points out that the *Encyclopedia Britannica* named the papacy as an ecclesiastical world empire, with papal ambassadors located in most nations of the world. Mr. Armstrong writes that he has nothing against Catholics but is concerned about Catholicism's relative political power, which can be seen as a dictatorship that is out to conquer the world.

Revelation 18:4–8

Revelation 18 continues as follows:

> *Then I heard another voice from heaven say: "'Come out of her, my people,' so that you will not share in her sins, so that you will not receive any of her plagues; for her*

> *sins are piled up to heaven, and God has remembered her crimes.* Give back to her as she has given; pay her back double for what she has done. Pour her a double portion from her own cup. Give her as much torment and grief as the glory and luxury she gave herself. *In her heart she boasts, 'I sit enthroned as queen. I am not a widow; I will never mourn.'* Therefore in one day her plagues will overtake her: death, mourning and famine. She will be consumed by fire, for mighty is the Lord God who judges her." (Revelation 18:4–8, emphasis added)

God calls any and all who would not share Satan's view to come out before He sends His wrath on this city and world system. Atheists, liberals, unrepentant non-believers, gays, lesbians, evildoers, and all others who would defy God will remain to be consumed by God's wrath.

Revelation 18:9–14

Revelation 18 continues as follows:

> When the kings of the earth who committed adultery with her and shared her luxury see the smoke of her burning, they will weep and mourn over her. Terrified at her torment, they will stand far off and cry: "Woe! Woe to you, great city, you mighty city of Babylon! In one hour your doom has come!" *The merchants of the earth will weep and mourn over her because no one buys their cargoes anymore—cargoes of gold, silver, precious stones and pearls; fine linen, purple, silk and scarlet cloth; every sort of citron wood, and articles of every kind made of ivory, costly wood, bronze, iron and marble; cargoes of cinnamon and spice, of incense, myrrh and frankincense, of wine and olive oil, of fine flour and wheat; cattle and sheep; horses and carriages; and human beings sold as slaves.* They will say, "The fruit you longed for is gone from you. All your luxury

and splendor have vanished, never to be recovered."
(Revelation 18:9–14, emphasis added)

We see the finest and best luxury items described here. This system of power has many riches to entice and enhance the world, but all will be gone when God decides to end these wordly desires that have misled humankind.

Revelation 18:15–19

Revelation 18 continues as follows:

> The merchants who sold these things and gained their wealth from her will stand far off, terrified at her torment. They will weep and mourn and cry out: "Woe! Woe to you, great city, dressed in fine linen, purple and scarlet, and glittering with gold, precious stones and pearls! In one hour such great wealth has been brought to ruin!" *Every sea captain, and all who travel by ship, the sailors, and all who earn their living from the sea, will stand far off. When they see the smoke of her burning, they will exclaim, "Was there ever a city like this great city?"* They will throw dust on their heads, and with weeping and mourning cry out: "Woe! Woe to you, great city, where all who had ships on the sea became rich through her wealth! In one hour she has been brought to ruin!" (Revelation 18:15–19, emphasis added)

From the above verses, we see the ruination of the whole world's political and economic systems of power and the people who controlled them. *This city or perhaps world system has to be one where boat-transported goods are very visible.* This might suggest cities like New York, London, and Tokyo, where shipping personnel are able to easily view these cities. This could also possibly mean many different cities around the world. We just *do not know* all of Revelation's meanings.

Revelation 18:20–24

Revelation 18 concludes with the following:

> *"Rejoice over her, you heavens! Rejoice, you people of God! Rejoice, apostles and prophets! For God has judged her with the judgment she imposed on you."* Then a mighty angel picked up a boulder the size of a large millstone and threw it into the sea, and said: "With such violence the great city of Babylon will be thrown down, never to be found again. The music of harpists and musicians, pipers and trumpeters, will never be heard in you again. No worker of any trade will ever be found in you again. The sound of a millstone will never be heard in you again. The light of a lamp will never shine in you again. *The voice of bridegroom and bride will never be heard in you again.* Your merchants were the world's important people. By your magic spell all the nations were led astray. *In her was found the blood of prophets and of God's holy people, of all who have been slaughtered on the earth."* (Revelation 18:20–24, emphasis added)

Finally, the destruction will be complete. Again, Babylon is presumably characteristic of whatever city or systems Babylon represents. Perhaps that devastation will occur by the great earthquake described in Revelation 16:18. The verse says, "Then there came flashes of lightning, rumblings, peals of thunder and a severe earthquake. No earthquake like it has ever occurred since mankind has been on earth, so tremendous was the quake." All those who have accepted Jesus as Savior will rejoice to see Satan's defeat in his attempt to take over God's world.

* * * * *

Revelation 19 brings us to the end of the great tribulation and hails God for defeating Satan and his followers at Armageddon. This is not the last battle fought on earth, but it may be one of the bloodiest. The last battle or final war takes place after the millennium, when God defeats Satan and his resurgent army. God casts them all into the lake of burning sulfur for eternity.

We now see heavenly visions and God praised as "the wedding supper of the Lamb" takes place.

Revelation 19:1–6

Revelation 19 begins as follows:

> After this I heard what sounded like the roar of a great multitude in heaven shouting: *"Hallelujah! Salvation and glory and power belong to our God, for true and just are his judgments.* He has condemned the great prostitute who corrupted the earth by her adulteries. He has avenged on her the blood of his servants." And again they shouted: "Hallelujah! The smoke from her goes up for ever and ever." *The twenty-four elders and the four living creatures fell down and worshiped God, who was seated on the throne. And they cried: "Amen, Hallelujah!" Then a voice came from the throne, saying:* "Praise our God, all you his servants, you who fear him, both great and small!" Then I heard what sounded like a great multitude, like the roar of rushing waters and like loud peals of thunder, shouting: *"Hallelujah! For our Lord God Almighty reigns."* (Revelation 19:1–6, emphasis added)

This "great multitude" is believed to be those who were saved during the great tribulation. The word *alleluia* ("hallelujah") comes from a composite of two Hebrew words, *hallel* and *jah* and is an adoring exclamation meaning "praise the Lord."

Revelation 19:7–10

Revelation 19 continues as follows:

> *Let us rejoice and be glad and give him glory! For the wedding of the Lamb has come, and his bride has made herself ready.* Fine linen, bright and clean, was given her to wear." (Fine linen stands for the righteous acts of God's holy people.) Then the angel said to me, "Write this: *Blessed are those who are invited to the wedding supper of the Lamb!*" And he added, "These are the true words of God." At this I fell at his feet to worship him. But he said to me, "Don't do that! I am a fellow servant with you and with your brothers and sisters who hold to the testimony of Jesus. *Worship God! For it is the Spirit of prophecy who bears testimony to Jesus.*" (Revelation 19:7–10, emphasis added)

The mental picture in this vision is one of a beautiful wedding. The Bible has expressed an image of Jesus and His church being united in marriage. The Hebrew people, in Scripture, are always represented as God's wife, but Christ Jesus's church is always seen as *His* bride. These verses envision believers' marriage to their creator, Jesus, who redeemed them from an eternal Hell in the lake of sulfur.

> Relatedly, Isaiah tells of the Jews, Israel, being called back to their "husband": "*For your Maker is your husband—the LORD Almighty is his name—the Holy One of Israel is your Redeemer*; he is called the God of all the earth. *The LORD will call you back as if you were a wife deserted and distressed in spirit—a wife who married young, only to be rejected*," says your God. "For a brief moment I abandoned you, but with deep compassion I will bring you back" (Isaiah 54:5–7, emphasis added).

Hosea's words further depict Israel's betrothal: "I will betroth you to me forever; I will betroth you in righteousness and justice, in love and compassion. I will betroth you in faithfulness, and you will acknowledge the LORD" (Hosea 2:19–20).

It is believed that the Jews will have their meeting with God after He returns to them, at the last real battle at Armageddon, because Zechariah 12:1–6 tells us,

> A prophecy: The word of the LORD concerning Israel. The LORD, who stretches out the heavens, who lays the foundation of the earth, and who forms the human spirit within a person, declares: "I am going to make Jerusalem a cup that sends all the surrounding peoples reeling. Judah will be besieged as well as Jerusalem. On that day, when all the nations of the earth are gathered against her, I will make Jerusalem an immovable rock for all the nations. All who try to move it will injure themselves. On that day I will strike every horse with panic and its rider with madness," declares the LORD. "I will keep a watchful eye over Judah, but I will blind all the horses of the nations. Then the clans of Judah will say in their hearts, 'The people of Jerusalem are strong, because the LORD Almighty is their God.' On that day I will make the clans of Judah like a firepot in a woodpile, like a flaming torch among sheaves. They will consume all the surrounding peoples right and left, but Jerusalem will remain intact in her place."

Zechariah 13:8–9 further helps us understand this: "In the whole land,... two-thirds will be struck down and perish; yet one-third will be left in it. This third I will put into the fire; I will refine them like silver and test them like gold. They will call on my name and I will answer them; I will say, 'They are my people,' and they will say, 'The LORD is our God.'"

And, again, Zechariah 12:10 explains, "And I will pour out on the house of David and the inhabitants of Jerusalem a spirit of grace and supplication. *They will look on me, the one they have pierced, and they will mourn for him as one mourns for an only child, and grieve bitterly for him as one grieves for a firstborn son*" (emphasis added). When that day comes, Satan and evil, degenerate people will attack Jerusalem. Jesus will show Himself to the Jewish people who are left. This *one-third* will be terribly tried by God so that they may gain His heaven.

Revelation 19:11–16

Revelation 19 continues as follows:

> *I saw heaven standing open and there before me was a white horse, whose rider is called Faithful and True.* With justice he judges and wages war. His eyes are like blazing fire, and on his head are many crowns. He has a name written on him that no one knows but he himself. *He is dressed in a robe dipped in blood, and his name is the Word of God.* The armies of heaven were following him, riding on white horses and dressed in fine linen, white and clean. Coming out of his mouth is a sharp sword with which to strike down the nations. "He will rule them with an iron scepter." He treads the winepress of the fury of the wrath of God Almighty. *On his robe and on his thigh he has this name written: KING OF KINGS AND LORD OF LORDS.* (Revelation 19:11–16, emphasis added)

This white horse's rider is the Lord going forth as a warrior into battle. Christ's robe is dipped either in the blood of His enemies or in His own blood from the cross. This would be fitting, because Jesus conquered death and hell for us on the cross. Only Jesus holds the keys to life.

This passage tells us that His name is the "Word of God." *Word* is capitalized and can only mean the Lord Jesus Christ. *Word* appears in the Bible 572 times. However, it is only capitalized six times, when it describes our Lord and Savior. These six capitalized instances are as follows:

> In the beginning was the *Word*, and the *Word* was with God, and the *Word* was God. (John 1:1, emphasis added)

The *Word* became flesh and made his dwelling among us. We have seen his glory, the glory of the one and only Son, who came from the Father, full of grace and truth. (John 1:14, emphasis added)

That which was from the beginning, which we have heard, which we have seen with our eyes, which we have looked at and our hands have touched—this we proclaim concerning the *Word* of life. (1 John 1:1, emphasis added)

He is dressed in a robe dipped in blood, and his name is the *Word* of God. (Revelation 19:13, emphasis added)

Revelation 19:17–21

Revelation 19 continues as follows:

And I saw an angel standing in the sun, who cried in a loud voice to all the birds flying in midair, "Come, gather together for the great supper of God, so that you may eat the flesh of kings, generals, and the mighty, of horses and their riders, and the flesh of all people, free and slave, great and small." Then I saw the beast and the kings of the earth and their armies gathered together to wage war against the rider on the horse and his army. But the beast was captured, and with it the false prophet who had performed the signs on its behalf. With these signs he had deluded those who had received the mark of the beast and worshiped its image. The two of them were thrown alive into the fiery lake of burning sulfur. The rest were killed with the sword coming out of the mouth of the rider on the horse, and all the birds gorged themselves on their flesh. (Revelation 19:17–21, emphasis added)

We see here a somewhat grim contrast to the wedding supper of the Lamb, but God is justified in His wrath. These people do not want anything to do with God, their creator. They desire to leave Him out and not only disobey but also sacrilegiously condemn Him.

Ezekiel prophesies this event for us:

> Son of man, this is what the Sovereign LORD says: Call out to every kind of bird and all the wild animals: "Assemble and come together from all around to the sacrifice I am preparing for you, the great sacrifice on the mountains of Israel. There you will eat flesh and drink blood. You will eat the flesh of mighty men and drink the blood of the princes of the earth as if they were rams and lambs, goats and bulls—all of them fattened animals from Bashan. At the sacrifice I am preparing for you, you will eat fat till you are glutted and drink blood till you are drunk. At my table you will eat your fill of horses and riders, mighty men and soldiers of every kind," declares the Sovereign LORD. (Ezekiel 39:17–20)

* * * * *

The twentieth chapter of Revelation describes some of the one-thousand-year period during which Satan will bound. This will be an unprecedented era of peace, justice, righteousness, joy, and prosperity for all who live on earth, because believers will be with Jesus, and He will rule.

This is what Isaiah, son of Amos, saw concerning Judah and Jerusalem:

> This is what Isaiah son of Amoz saw concerning Judah and Jerusalem: *In the last days the mountain of the LORD's temple will be established as the highest of the mountains; it will be exalted above the hills, and all nations will stream to it. Many peoples will come and say, "Come, let us go up to the mountain of the LORD, to the temple of the God of Jacob.* He will teach us his ways, so that we may walk in his paths." *The law will go out from Zion, the word of the LORD from Jerusalem.* He will judge between the nations and will settle disputes

for many peoples. They will beat their swords into plowshares and their spears into pruning hooks. Nation will not take up sword against nation, nor will they train for war anymore. (Isaiah 2:1–4, emphasis added)

Jesus will be completely in charge and only good and righteousness will be done on earth. It will be an unprecedented time of harmony, affluence, and joy.

Revelation 20:1–3

Revelation 20:1–3 introduces us to Satan's one-thousand-year captivity: "And I saw an angel coming down out of heaven, having the key to the Abyss and holding in his hand a great chain. He seized the dragon, that ancient serpent, who is the devil, or Satan, and bound him for a thousand years. He threw him into the Abyss, and locked and sealed it over him, to keep him from deceiving the nations anymore until the thousand years were ended. After that, he must be set free for a short time." This angel, having the keys to the abyss and a great chain, might be Michael, the archangel of God. Michael was powerful enough to restrain Satan in the past, and Satan would be strong and surely resist. About Michael, God said to Daniel, "At that time Michael, the great prince who protects your people, will arise. There will be a time of distress such as has not happened from the beginning of nations until then. But at that time your people—everyone whose name is found written in the book—will be delivered" (Daniel 12:1).

Because of the events mentioned above, it is believed by many Bible students that we have definitely seen the unsealing of the scroll, which places mankind in the end times. There are three basic opinions regarding the one- thousand-year period. These three opinions are known as *a millennialism, pre millennialism,* and *post millennialism.* These views are described in the preface. For our purposes, it is important to know that Jesus Christ reigns for the one-thousand-year period, after which time Satan will be released.

Revelation 20:4–6

Revelation 20 continues as follows:

> I saw thrones on which were seated those who had been given authority to judge. *And I saw the souls of those who had been beheaded because of their testimony about Jesus and because of the word of God.* They had not worshiped the beast or its image and had not received its mark on their foreheads or their hands. *They came to life and reigned with Christ a thousand years.* (The rest of the dead did not come to life until the thousand years were ended.) This is the first resurrection. Blessed and holy are those who share in the first resurrection. The second death has no power over them, but they will be priests of God and of Christ and will reign with him for a thousand years. (Revelation 20:4–6, emphasis added)

God's chosen people, especially the martyred ones who were beheaded, will apparently reign with Christ during the one-thousand-year period when Satan is bound. "The rest of the dead" may refer to those who had been martyred for Jesus.

About God's people, the Bible has said, "Or do you not know that the Lord's people will judge the world? And if you are to judge the world, are you not competent to judge trivial cases?" (1 Corinthians 6:2). Another relevant verse comes from 2 Timothy: "Here is a trustworthy saying: If we died with him, we will also live with him; if we endure, we will also reign with him. If we disown him, he will also disown us" (2 Timothy 2:11–12).

Revelation 20:7–10

Revelation 20 continues:

> *When the thousand years are over, Satan will be released from his prison and will go out to deceive the nations in the four corners of the earth—Gog and Magog—and*

> *to gather them for battle.* In number they are like the sand on the seashore. They marched across the breadth of the earth and surrounded the camp of God's people, the city he loves. But fire came down from heaven and devoured them. And the devil, who deceived them, was thrown into the lake of burning sulfur, where the beast and the false prophet had been thrown. They will be tormented day and night for ever and ever. (Revelation 20:7–10, emphasis added)

It seems difficult to understand why God would release Satan after one thousand years. However, God knows that there are certain people who would still want to be with Satan and rebel. God gives these people one more chance to choose. *With Satan released, people will still be deceived and turn to him, even though they will have lived under Jesus's reign for one thousand years.* We might conjecture that some of these people may have been born in the one-thousand-year period and, although having lived under Jesus Christ's government, will not want to be ruled by God. They will rebel, just as humankind has been doing for the thousands of years, from Adam to the rapture. This will be the last battle on earth, and Satan and his followers will be totally defeated by God. Satan and his followers will be thrown into the lake of burning sulfur to be tormented eternally.

As was indicated earlier, because human beings have the freedom to think, we make our own choices. The important thing is that *you* make the right choice!

Revelation 20:11–15

The next five verses further reveal Revelation's prophecy.

> Then I saw a great white throne and him who was seated on it. The earth and the heavens fled from his presence, and there was no place for them. *And I saw the dead, great and small, standing before the throne, and books were opened. Another book was opened,*

which is the book of life. The dead were judged according to what they had done as recorded in the books. The sea gave up the dead that were in it, and death and Hades gave up the dead that were in them, and *each person was judged according to what they had done. Then death and Hades were thrown into the lake of fire. The lake of fire is the second death.* Anyone whose name was not found written in the book of life was thrown into the lake of fire. (Revelation 20:11–15, emphasis added)

These verses reveal for us the great white judgment throne, with Jesus seated to judge all of humankind. *Human beings will be judged according to their deeds and whether or not they chose to receive Jesus as Lord and Savior.* As the Bible says, "For just as the Father raises the dead and gives them life, even so *the Son gives life to whom he is pleased to give it.* Moreover, the Father judges no one, but has entrusted all judgment to the Son, that all may honor the Son just as they honor the Father. *Whoever does not honor the Son does not honor the Father, who sent him*" (John 5:21–23, emphasis added).

We also read in the Old Testament, "I the LORD search the heart and examine the mind, to reward each person according to their conduct, according to what their deeds deserve" (Jeremiah 17:10).

* * * * *

The next two chapters of Revelation reveal the new heaven and earth, with a new holy city, which is the New Jerusalem brought down for Christ's church, His bride, to live in. From here on, God will live with His people.

Revelation 21:1–4

Chapter 21 introduces us to this beautiful future.

> *Then I saw "a new heaven and a new earth," for the first heaven and the first earth had passed away, and there was no longer any sea. I saw the Holy City, the new Jerusalem, coming down out of heaven from God, prepared as a bride beautifully dressed for her husband. And I heard a loud voice from the throne saying, "Look! God's dwelling place is now among the people, and he will dwell with them. They will be his people, and God himself will be with them and be their God. 'He will wipe every tear from their eyes. There will be no more death' or mourning or crying or pain, for the old order of things has passed away."* (Revelation 21:1–4, emphasis added)

There will no longer be a sea or a first earth. We do not know if the first earth will be consumed by fire or just disappear, and we do not know if a new earth will be created, but *we will live with God in the New Jerusalem.* The very thought of God Himself dwelling with humankind is awesome! Living with God means no more pain, suffering, mourning, death, sin—nothing but joy, happiness, righteousness, purity, holiness, and life eternal.

There has always been speculation about what we would be doing in heaven for eternity, but some Bible scholars think we will be in service to God, fulfilling His plans for the universe. Genesis gives us an inkling that something had (possibly) happened to God's universe between verse one and two. (This is known as the "gap theory.") God would not create anything dark or foreboding. God only creates beauty. The answer *may* be that sin corrupted God's universe, everything God had made, including humankind.

The gap theory (if true) hints at a once-beautiful universe made barren by sin. *If* this theory is correct, given the universe's billions of stars and planets, several verses in the Bible seem to indicate that God has always planned to inhabit His universe. Perhaps *we*, as Jesus's brothers and sisters, will somehow be of service to make

God's wondrous creation, the universe, beautiful again. Consider the following: "I have put my words in your mouth and covered you with the shadow of my hand—I who set the heavens in place, who laid the foundations of the earth, and who say to Zion, 'You are my people'" (Isaiah 51:16). Isaiah also says, "For this is what the LORD says —he who created the heavens, he is God; he who fashioned and made the earth, he founded it; *he did not create it to be empty, but formed it to be inhabited*—he says: 'I am the LORD, and there is no other'" (Isaiah 45:19, emphasis added).

Revelation 21:5–8

Revelation 21 continues as follows:

> He who was seated on the throne said, "I am making everything new!" Then he said, "Write this down, for these words are trustworthy and true." He said to me: "It is done. I am the Alpha and the Omega, the Beginning and the End. To the thirsty I will give water without cost from the spring of the water of life. Those who are victorious will inherit all this, and I will be their God and they will be my children. But the cowardly, the unbelieving, the vile, the murderers, the sexually immoral, those who practice magic arts, the idolaters and all liars—they will be consigned to the fiery lake of burning sulfur. This is the second death." "In the greatness of your majesty you threw down those who opposed you. You unleashed your burning anger; it consumed them like stubble. (Revelation 21:5–8)

will have *a new city, Jerusalem, plus a new universe* to live in. It is possible that God's chosen ones will help in the rebuilding of the new universe.

As we read in Genesis, "In the beginning God created the heavens and the earth. *Now the earth was formless and empty, darkness was over the surface of the deep, and the Spirit of God was hovering over the waters*" (Genesis 1:1–2, emphasis added). There is scientific evidence that *after* God created everything, darkness prevailed for some time. (This, again, is the so-called gap theory.) The April 2014 issue of *Scientific American* had a report about the cosmos going dark shortly after the theorized "big bang" occurred. Although believers in God do *not* accept the Big Bang theory, we do accept scientific proofs and their findings *if* they reflect the truth of the Bible. This evidence *may* give some evidence for the Gap Theory, but it still is only a guess of what *might* have happened. The question is, was there a period of darkness, caused by sin, after the creation? Also, did God correct this situation by giving us light? Genesis 1:3–4 tells us, "And God said, 'Let there be light,' and there was light. God saw that the light was good, and he separated the light from the darkness."

The *Scientific American* article states, "[The] very first stars and planets were *not like* the objects we see today" (emphasis added).[1] They then explain their hypothesis and have a picture of cosmic history to show how the universe went dark shortly after their theory of the so-called "big bang." This darkness that lasted for some period of time could easily be construed as the darkness caused by sin, which God transforms with and into light.

In addition, this same article reports that scientists believe they have discovered that the universe is expanding. Scientists believe they have ascertained ripples or waves that indicate staggering exponential expansion that started during the incident immediately following the so-called big bang.[2] These waves or ripples are not the same as the normal inflation waves of the universe and, they say, are the first direct proof of the universe undergoing rapid expansion. During this period, particles inflated *faster than the speed of light*, leaving what the experts call "stretch marks" across the cosmos. These stretch marks validate our universe's continuous expansion since the beginning of time. Clearly, this scientific finding again authenticates and validates Scripture. "Stretch marks" are mentioned several times in the Bible, as *The Trumpet Magazine*[3] indicates.

> He spreads out the northern skies over empty space; he suspends the earth over nothing. (Job 26:7)

It is I who made the earth and created mankind on it. My own hands stretched out the heavens; I marshaled their starry hosts. (Isaiah 45:12)

But God made the earth by his power; he founded the world by his wisdom and stretched out the heavens by his understanding. (Jeremiah 10:12)

One interesting point is that science, at first, *rejected* the big bang theory, because it seemed too religious.

Scientific findings indicate *there is no disagreement between science and Scripture*, but there are *significant differences* between some scientific *theory* and Scripture. I believe the universe is infinite, because God is infinite! Scientists argue the big bang theory, which is based on mathematics and takes the universe back to a single point the size of an electron or smaller. To my thinking, this is *zero*, which means the universe is infinite, but they refuse to believe infinity is possible. Someday, we may know the answer when we ask God Himself. I do not know if scientists will ever know the answer.

Revelation 21:9–13

Revelation 21:9–13 reads as follows:

One of the seven angels who had the seven bowls full of the seven last plagues came and said to me, "Come, I will show you the bride, the wife of the Lamb." And he carried me away in the Spirit to a mountain great and high, and showed me the Holy City, Jerusalem, coming down out of heaven from God. It shone with the glory of God, and its brilliance was like that of a very precious jewel, like a jasper, clear as crystal. It had a great, high wall with twelve gates, and with twelve angels at the gates. On the gates were written the names of the twelve tribes of Israel. There were three gates on the east, three on the north, three on the south and three on the west.

John is transported away in the spirit to view the Lamb's wife and the New Jerusalem that is lighted by God Himself.

The New Jerusalem will be a beautiful, glorified city, in which those who have received Jesus as Lord will live with Christ Jesus for one thousand years.

Revelation shows us that John was in heaven when he had this vision, because he was in the Spirit.

Revelation 21:14–20

Revelation 21 continues as follows:

> The wall of the city had twelve foundations, and on them were the names of the twelve apostles of the Lamb. The angel who talked with me had a measuring rod of gold to measure the city, its gates and its walls. The city was laid out like a square, as long as it was wide. *He measured the city with the rod and found it to be 12,000 stadia in length, and as wide and high as it is long.* The angel measured *the wall using human measurement, and it was 144 cubits thick.* The wall was made of jasper, and the city of pure gold, as pure as glass. The foundations of the city walls were decorated with every kind of precious stone. The first foundation was jasper, the second sapphire, the third agate, the fourth emerald, the fifth onyx, the sixth ruby, the seventh chrysolite, the eighth beryl, the ninth topaz, the tenth turquoise, the eleventh jacinth, and the twelfth amethyst. (Revelation 21:14–20, emphasis added)

Just to give one an idea of the size of this city, one furlong equals 220 yards. Hence, twelve thousand furlongs equals 2,640,000 yards, with is fifteen hundred miles. Understand, this is the "length, breadth, and height," which are equal (and therefore form a cube). I assume that city could hold a great number of *spiritual beings* without crowding.

Precious beautiful stones comprise the making of the wall and surround will surround us when we are not admiring the Lord.

Revelation 21:21–27

Revelation 21 continues as follows:

> The twelve gates were twelve pearls, each gate made of a single pearl. The great street of the city was of gold, as pure as transparent glass. *I did not see a temple in the city, because the Lord God Almighty and the Lamb are its temple. The city does not need the sun or the moon to shine on it, for the glory of God gives it light, and the Lamb is its lamp.* The nations will walk by its light, and the kings of the earth will bring their splendor into it. On no day will its gates ever be shut, for there will be no night there. *The glory and honor of the nations will be brought into it. Nothing impure will ever enter it*, nor will anyone who does what is shameful or deceitful, but only those whose names are written in the Lamb's book of life. (Revelation 21:21–27, emphasis added)

The twelve gates are one pearl each. These pearl gates may symbolize and represent the church, because Jesus paid the *greatest price*. According to Matthew 13:45–46, "Again, the kingdom of heaven is like a merchant looking for fine pearls. When he found one of great value, he went away and sold everything he had and bought it." Only Jesus, now glorified, is the illumination in heaven.

The description of the city is fantastically beautiful with its golden streets and precious-stone walls. No defilement will ever enter this city of God.

* * * * *

Revelation 22 gives us the closing of this marvelous book. Understand that there is much more that is known and could be said by many scholarly people about Revelation. Read; study your Bible to see the wonder of God and His plan for your life.

Revelation 22:1–5

Revelation 22 shows us "the pure river of water of life, clear as crystal, proceeding from the throne of God and of the Lamb." Near this river, we see the tree of life bearing its twelve fruits. Psalm 46:4 tell us, "There is a river whose streams make glad the city of God, the holy place where the Most High dwells." These descriptions remind us of the garden of Eden, but we will actually be living in a garden-like *city*, with God.

According to the first verses of Revelation 22,

> Then the angel showed me the river of the water of life, as clear as crystal, flowing from the throne of God and of the Lamb down the middle of the great street of the city. *On each side of the river stood the tree of life, bearing twelve crops of fruit, yielding its fruit every month.* And the leaves of the tree are for the healing of the nations. No longer will there be any curse. *The throne of God and of the Lamb will be in the city, and his servants will serve him. They will see his face, and his name will be on their foreheads. There will be no more night. They will not need the light of a lamp or the light of the sun, for the Lord God will give them light. And they will reign for ever and ever.* (Revelation 22:1–5, emphasis added)

This suggests that we may indeed help to remake the universe to God's specifications. Our duties of judging angels and human beings will be included in the workload, so we will not be bored or just lying around doing nothing. Some human beings who were martyred for God will reign on earth with our Lord for one thousand years, as we have read previously. One can only assume that all will work for God for eternity doing His work.

Revelation 22:6–11

Revelation now begins its epilogue.

> The angel said to me, "These words are trustworthy and true. The Lord, the God who inspires the prophets, sent his angel to show his servants the things that must soon take place." *"Look, I am coming soon! Blessed is the one who keeps the words of the prophecy written in this scroll."* I, John, am the one who heard and saw these things. And when I had heard and seen them, I fell down to worship at the feet of the angel who had been showing them to me. he said to me, "Don't do that! I am a fellow servant with you and with your fellow prophets and with all who keep the words of this scroll. *Worship God*!" Then he told me, "Do not seal up the words of the prophecy of this scroll, because the time is near. Let the one who does wrong continue to do wrong; let the vile person continue to be vile; let the one who does right continue to do right; and let the holy person continue to be holy." (Revelation 22:6–11, emphasis added)

All of prophecy *will be fulfilled*. Jesus tells us in verse 7, "Blessed is the one who keeps the words of the prophecy written in this scroll." Jesus told us He is coming soon, and all the prophecy that has already been fulfilled leads us to believe it could happen any moment. John is told to not seal these words of prophecy, because *the time is near.*

Let those who do wrong continue to do wrong, but you remain true to God.

Are you ready for His coming?

Revelation 22:12–16

The epilogue continues,

> *"Look, I am coming soon! My reward is with me, and I will give to each person according to what they have*

done. I am the Alpha and the Omega, the First and the Last, the Beginning and the End. *"Blessed are those who wash their robes, that they may have the right to the tree of life and may go through the gates into the city.* Outside are the dogs, those who practice magic arts, the sexually immoral, the murderers, the idolaters and everyone who loves and practices falsehood. *"I, Jesus, have sent my angel to give you this testimony for the churches.* I am the Root and the Offspring of David, and the bright Morning Star." (Revelation 22:12–16, emphasis added)

"Blessed are those who wash their robes, that they may have the right to the tree of life" is the last beatitude given in the Bible. Take heart if you have received Jesus as Lord and Savior. Simply believe it! He is coming soon.

Only those saved by Jesus are allowed to go in and out of God's holy city.

Are you one of them?

Revelation 22:17–21

With the following verses, the epilogue, and the book itself, concludes:

> *The Spirit and the bride say, "Come!"* And let the one who hears say, "Come!" *Let the one who is thirsty come; and let the one who wishes take the free gift of the water of life I warn everyone who hears the words of the prophecy of this scroll*: If anyone adds anything to them, God will add to that person the plagues described in this scroll. And if anyone takes words away from this scroll of prophecy, God will take away from that person any share in the tree of life and in the Holy City, which are described in this scroll. He who testifies to these things says, *"Yes, I am coming soon."* Amen. Come,

Lord Jesus. The grace of the Lord Jesus be with God's people. Amen. (Revelation 22:17–21, emphasis added)

Do not toy with God's holy Word, but "come" to Him for His redeeming love and salvation.

The Bible and history record that God's Son, Jesus, came to earth to redeem humankind from our sins. Jesus lived a sinless life as half-man and half-God so that He would be the perfect sacrifice to pay for humankind's sins. The Bible says it this way: "My dear children, I write this to you so that you will not sin. But if anybody does sin, we have an advocate with the Father—*Jesus Christ, the Righteous One. He is the atoning sacrifice for our sins, and not only for ours but also for the sins of the whole world*" (1 John 2:1–2, emphasis added).

Also consider the following verses:

> *God presented Christ as a sacrifice of atonement [a propitiation] through the shedding of his blood—to be received by faith.* He did this to demonstrate his righteousness, because in his forbearance he had left the sins committed beforehand unpunished. (Romans 3:25, emphasis added)

> This is how God showed his love among us: He sent his one and only Son into the world that we might live through him. This is love: not that we loved God, but that he loved us and sent his Son as an atoning sacrifice for our sins. (1 John 4:9)

> This is love: not that we loved God, but that he loved us and sent his Son as an atoning sacrifice for our sins. (1 John 4:10)

To repeat myself, how does one achieve salvation and the forgiveness of sin? By *obeying God's wishes*, which are given throughout the Bible and particularly clearly spoken in Romans.

> If you *declare with your mouth, "Jesus is Lord," and believe in your heart that God raised him from the dead,*

you will be saved. For *it is with your heart that you believe and are justified, and it is with your mouth that you profess your faith and are saved.* As Scripture says, "Anyone who believes in him will never be put to shame." For there is *no difference between Jew and Gentile—the same Lord is Lord of all and richly blesses all who call on him, for,* "*Everyone who calls on the name of the Lord will be saved.* (Romans 10:9–13, emphasis added)

May God bless you for having read His book of Revelation.

* * * * *

Amen, amen, and amen.

Notes

Preface

1. Elmer Ubbink, 333 Specific Prophetic Details about the Lord Jesus Christ (Tyler, TX: Jewels Publishing, 1982).

1—Revelation 1:1–3:22

1. H.L.Willmington, Willmington's Guide to the Bible, Wheaton, IL:Tyndale House, 2011, 541.
2. Ibid, 541
3. Ibid, 543
4. Ibid, 543.
5. Ibid, 543–544.
6. John McClintock and James Strong, Cyclopedia of Biblical, Theological, and Ecclesiastical Literature (New York: Harper & Brothers, 1870) Volume 1, 174
7. Ibid. Volume 7, 547.
8. H.L.Willmington, Willmington's Guide to the Bible, Wheaton, IL: Tyndale House, 2011, 547

2—Revelation 4:1–11:19

1. Ibid., 552.
2. John McClintock and James Strong, Cyclopedia of Biblical, Theological, and Ecclesiastical Literature. (New York: Harper & Brothers, 1870) Volume 1, 57

3—Revelation 12:1–13:18

1. Willmington, Willmington's Guide to the Bible,. (Wheaton, IL: Tyndale House, 2011) 564

5—Revelation 18:1–22:21

1. M.D, Lemonick, Scientific American, April 2014, 38
2. Ibid. 38
3. Jeremiah Jaques, The Philadelphia Trumpet, May-June, 2014, 7.

www.ingramcontent.com/pod-product-compliance
Lightning Source LLC
LaVergne TN
LVHW091555060526
838200LV00036B/854